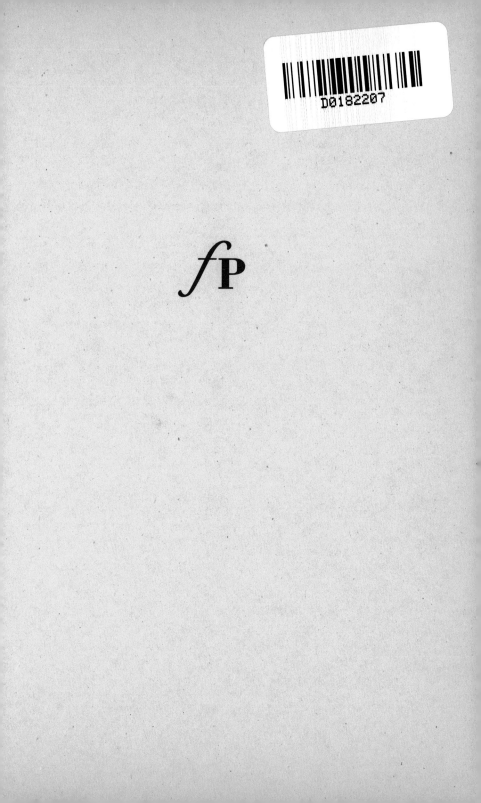

fP

THE
LAWS *of*
MONEY

---

5 Timeless Secrets to
Get Out and Stay Out
of Financial Trouble

SUZE
ORMAN

fP

FREE PRESS

New York   London   Toronto   Sydney

This publication contains the opinions and ideas of its author. It is intended to provide helpful and informative material on the subjects addressed in the publication. It is sold with the understanding that the author and publisher are not engaged in rendering legal, accounting, or any other kind of personal professional services in the book. The reader should consult a competent professional for legal, financial, or other professional advice or before adopting any of the suggestions in this book or drawing inferences from it.

The author and publisher specifically disclaim all responsibility for any liability, loss or risk, personal or otherwise, which is incurred as a consequence, directly or indirectly, of the use and application of any of the contents of this book.

FREE PRESS
A Division of Simon & Schuster Inc.
1230 Avenue of the Americas
New York, NY 10020

People First, Then Money, Then Things® is a federally
registered trademark owned by Suze Orman.

First Free Press trade paperback edition 2004

FREE PRESS and colophon are trademarks
of Simon & Schuster, Inc.

For information about special discounts for bulk purchases,
please contact Simon & Schuster Special Sales at
1-800-456-6798 or business@simonandschuster.com

Designed by Nancy Singer Olaguera

Manufactured in the United States of America

10 9 8 7 6 5 4 3 2 1

Library of Congress Cataloging-in-Publication Data is available.

ISBN 0-7432-4517-2
      0-7432-4518-0(Pbk)

*This book is dedicated to the one
who is always the first to start clapping
and the last to stop!*

ACKNOWLEDGMENTS

As I write these acknowledgments, it is 5:00 A.M. in New York and I have just sent off the last chapter of this book to my editor, Leslie Meredith. It is quiet—the city is not yet awake. It is my favorite time of day to think and write.

My thoughts this morning are with the many devoted people who have helped me to create and produce *The Laws of Money*. Most are the very same people I started with more than seven years ago, when I wrote and published my first books. I am grateful and proud that they remain part of my life today.

I am also in a state of amazement that this is my sixth book and that millions and millions of copies later you, the reader, remain with me too.

So the first acknowledgment goes to you, the reader of my books. I thank you for your ongoing support of my work and for your intention to keep facing your finances with integrity, faith, and courage.

Next, I want to thank Amanda (Binky) Urban, my literary agent. When my publishing career was just really beginning, I did not understand what a book agent did, let alone why I would need one. I have since learned just how valuable a good literary agent can be. Binky is the best. From the first time I saw her, I knew that she was right for me. It was as if I were picking a stock that I thought would be a good investment for the long run—and I was right. Binky is one of the best investments I have ever made.

Cheryl Merser, who was one of the first writers I ever worked with, has continued to write with me and has worked on almost every one of my books. To write a book with someone is not an easy task, and most collaborations last for only one or possibly two books. Cheryl and I not only love working with each other still to this day, we love each other tremendously, and Cheryl has become more than just part of my writing. She has become a big part of my heart. Cheryl, I know you know.

About Karen Fonner, director of brands for QVC television, I can only say, Wow! What a woman! Karen pioneered my work on QVC and as a result I have accomplished things that, without her, never could have happened. She has been with me for almost every one of my shows and is the person I consider my good luck charm. The publication of this book will mark my ninth year on QVC. I have loved every one of those years, and the number one reason I have loved them is Karen. She is now one of my dearest and closest friends. I really do not have words to describe my complete affection for this woman.

Sandi Mendelson is my publicist. After I began to believe that maybe, just maybe, I was not simply a financial advisor but was also about to become an author, Binky introduced me to Sandi, and I am so very, very glad she did. Sandi is a wonderful publicist and has also, over the years, become the grounding force for everything I do. She understands me—a rare treat in any life. She understands my message and its importance. All the money in the world could never buy anything that could replace her friendship and loyalty. For this I am grateful.

My entry into writing for magazines started in 1997 with my compadre Anne Heller and has continued over all these years to my books as well as my newsletter. I call her my intellectual better half, for Anne has one of the most precise minds with which I have ever come into contact. Anne always questions my concepts and makes sure that I am saying what I mean to say. When you couple intellect with a love of the word, which Anne has, you have a writer who is a true, priceless treasure.

Mary Bourn, my personal assistant, is the person who has been my behind-the-scenes support, helping me in every possible way. She has been my road warrior—traveling on all my book tours, and to my PBS specials and speaking engagements, here and in South Africa—and has made managing my frantic schedule seem almost easy. But the main gift Mary brings into my life is laughter; the moment I see her, my life lights up. Mary is a breath of fresh air. Her presence helps me never to forget what is important in life. I have met many people, but Mary is among those who bring me the greatest joy.

From the first deal that I struck back in 1996, Ken Browning, my lawyer, has been by my side, and he grows more important to me as the years go on—as both a colleague and a friend. I rely on him in my business dealings, and I also count on him as one of my favorite people. In a world that is seemingly so harsh when it comes to business dealings, it is a gift for me to know that I can depend on Ken.

Carol Bruckner, my speaking agent, is the wizard behind the curtain of my public appearances. I travel the world speaking, and to this day it shocks me that I get paid handsomely to do so, for it is one of the things I most love to do. It is here that I get to meet my readers and listeners face-to-face, and I cherish the encounters. Carol makes that happen. Again, Carol and I have become dear friends. When I am speaking, it comforts me to know that I have my invisible wizard and friend by my side.

Along with every book there seems to come a PBS special. To make those specials happen is far from easy. The man who makes them happen is Gerry Richman, executive vice president of national productions at Twin Cities Public Television, a kind soul who has devoted many hours of work to helping me bring money magic to PBS audiences nationwide. I thank him with all my heart.

Kristin Bouton, who started working with me almost from day one, is my buddy first and my product development person second. There is no one as thorough, competent in her field, and creative as Kristin. As I give birth to this, my sixth book, Kristin gave birth to her first child. May they both grow to be all that we wish for them.

Attorney Janet Dobrovolny is my expert in trust-and-estate planning and one of my oldest and dearest friends. I stand in amazement at the extraordinary energy and expertise she brings to the world and to my life. How do you acknowledge someone who for more than twenty years has been one of the forces behind one's every breath? There are no words, Janet, just love.

To Kathy Travis, a branding genius who has put together an unprecedented national bus tour to launch this book as well as managed a million other projects and ideas for me, I offer heart-felt thanks. K.T., as I call her, is brilliant and modest. She is the brains behind the look and feel of all that I do. She brings a smile to my heart every time I see her, and this is true for everyone who meets her. The world is a better place because K.T. is in it and as we all say about our K.T., she is Pure Goodness.

Twenty years ago, when I worked for Prudential Bache Securities, Preston Cranford was my manager. He now runs an internet university and manages my website. Preston and his crew take care of an average of over eight million readers and browsers who visit my site each month. He is also my friend.

Many years ago I started a journey to learn the answer to the question, Who am I? What is the goal of life? Laura Duggan, one of my dearest and wisest friends, has been a voyager on that journey with me now for as long as I can remember. Whenever I have had a question she has been there to help me find the answer, and we have spent countless hours exploring the unknowns of life. Laura discussed every word of this book as it was forming and helped to make sure that there was absolute truth behind all the laws in this book. I love you, my dearest Laura, and may this year bring you the answers you are looking for.

There are many more people to thank: my newest writer, Deb DeFord, who helped create the guidebook at the end of this book; Carla Fried, a brilliant writer and copyeditor and a sheer delight to work with; all the people who have supported me through the years, including Nancy Friend, Judy Hilsinger, and Martha Craig of Hilsinger Mendelson; the wonderful people at QVC, including Alan Massaro, my producer, and MaryAnn Shumbo, my director, along with Darlene Daggett, Mary Campbell, John Kelly, Doug Thompson, Mark Wennersten, and Amy Corey; Amy Feller, my executive producer for *The Suze Orman Show* at CNBC, whom I adore; Pamela Thomas-Graham, president and chief executive officer, CNBC; Cheryl Gould, NBC news vice president for CNBC prime-time and weekend programming; Lauren Donovan, senior vice president and general counsel, NBC Cable; Cornelia Kohl, the producer of my former radio show; all those with whom I work closely at *O, The Oprah Magazine*, Amy Gross, editor-in-chief, Jill D. Seelig, publisher, Karen Frank, photo director, and Catherine Gunderson, associate editor, and the other great editors and production staff that make that magazine so worthwhile; and to Elizabeth Flowers whose very own story inspired much of this book.

In the end, in order for this book to come to life it took the work of a slew of dedicated people at the Free Press. To the publisher of the Free Press, Martha Levin, I extend my thanks for bearing with this project in such an open way. And I offer additional thanks to Carolyn Reidy, president of Simon and Schuster's Adult Publishing Group. Also at the Free Press, I thank Dominick Anfuso, the editorial director and a prince among men; Leslie Meredith, my editor, with whom I loved working, and my own personal LMLL; Suzanne Donahue, associate publisher; Susan Fleming-Holland, vice president and director of marketing; Mark Speer, director of advertising and promotion; Carisa Hays, publicity director; and all the people behind the scenes from the designers to the printers. At Simon and Schuster Audio, thanks to Susan Perrin, who really is the most extraordinary audio producer with whom I have ever worked, and to Michael Jones, who was engineer extraordinaire. What a great time we had.

For all of you who know how much you mean to me, and your name is not here, know that you have not gone unacknowledged in my heart, for this whole book really could be filled with just your names alone, so please know I thank all the ones who have not been named individually, but you know who you are.

Finally, of course, I offer loving acknowledgment to my mom, who is the source of all my success and who knows that I love her more than life itself.

CONTENTS

THE LAWS OF MONEY GUIDEBOOK

Introduction: Letting Out the Secrets

———

One day the news of an impending hurricane went sweeping through a seaside town. As the winds were picking up and the tide rising, the authorities rushed from door to door, instructing the residents to evacuate, to pack up their valuables and head inland. All of the townspeople—except for one—did as advised, acting as fast as they could, loading their cars with their family photographs, TVs, clothes, cash, and their most important records and documents. Most were well inland by the time the torrential rains began hitting their town. Only one man stayed behind, saying calmly to the authorities as they knocked on his door, "No, I'll be okay. God will take care of me."

As the town started to flood, with water swirling waist high, a boat with a rescue team made its way to the man's house, urging him to climb on board and get to safety. Again the man said confidently, "No, I'll be okay. God will take care of me."

Soon the rising waters submerged almost all the houses in the town and the man found himself stranded on his rooftop. A Coast Guard helicopter appeared, and lowered a ladder for the man to climb to safety. Again he refused, calling out, "No, I'll be okay. God will take care of me." It was his last chance. Within an hour the floodwaters engulfed the house, drowning the man.

Upon reaching heaven, the man, totally confused and feeling utterly betrayed, appeared in front of God and asked, "Why did you not take care of me and save me from the storm?" God replied, "I did try to take care of you. I sent you a messenger, a lifeboat, and a helicopter! What more did you want me to do?"

What more, indeed?

FIVE TIMELESS LAWS OF MONEY, FIVE SECRETS

When I travel the country, I am saddened to see the faces of all the people who have gotten into serious financial trouble. They are smart people, good people, kind people. So what happened?

The answer is really very simple. These people, just like the man in our parable, did not know the financial signs they needed to pay attention to when they appeared in front of them. They did not know what to do with their money and when to do it.

Let's get real; the person who I am talking about is you. You—like most people—don't even like to think about the financial what-ifs of life, let alone talk freely about your money. You, like many people, probably feel that the topic of money is so personal that it needs to be kept tucked away like a deep dark secret. And because you treat money as a secret, you don't have the opportunity to discover the Laws of Money.

And that is where your trouble begins: Even though you don't know about a law, you can still end up breaking it. And your ignorance of the law doesn't get you off the hook. You still suffer the consequences if you break it.

Think of a well-known law that is posted and straight-forward—for instance, the highway speed limit is 55 miles per hour; that's the law. You know very well in that case when you are breaking the law and when you are not, for there are reminders of that law every few miles. That is why when you are speeding and breaking the law, you are constantly looking in the rearview mirror to make sure you do not get caught. At least in this case you are aware that you are breaking the law, and if you get caught, you have no one to blame but yourself.

But when it comes to money, there are no huge signs con-stantly posted along your path to tell you how fast to go, when to yield, or even when to stop. So you are often breaking the laws of money and just don't know it. But, even worse, you have no idea of the consequences you will suffer if you break a law of money. And when you do break a law of money, the end result makes you feel as if you are in financial prison—you have less money, more debt, and no security. When you know the laws of money and follow them, however, you will be able to create more money, get out of debt, and increase your personal freedom.

DON'T GIVE UP—YOU WILL DO IT!

So many people have been greatly affected by the volatile econ-omy of the recent past. It's likely you have, too. Maybe you have worked hard all of your life and now, just as the promise of retirement approaches, find that much or all of your money you so carefully saved has disappeared. Maybe you invested your time and money in what you thought were no-lose propositions, but you did lose—big-time; it may take you years to recover your losses and years more to get ahead. Perhaps you lost your job and are having trouble finding another. Or possibly you are just simply overburdened with mortgage debt, car loan debt, credit card debt or student loans, and you don't see a way ever to get above water; your financial stance is, Why should I even try?

This is what I want you to remember: Every person I talk to who is in financial trouble would have benefited from knowing the five laws of money that I reveal in this book. Even though every person's financial situation is unique, the laws of money are universal. Even if you have made some bad investments or gotten in over your head with your credit cards, these laws will lead you back to a trouble-free plan for your money. All you have to do to start is to read this book from cover to cover.

THE LAWS OF MONEY ARE TRUTHS THAT WILL ALWAYS GUIDE YOU TO TAKE THE CORRECT FINANCIAL ACTIONS

Is it really that easy? You bet. Listen, there will be many times in your life when you look back and say, "If I only knew then what I know now. . . ." In some cases, only time and experience could have served as your teacher and you had to make mistakes to learn. But when it comes to money, I believe from the bottom of my heart it does not have to be that way. If you want to get out and stay out of trouble with your money—and who doesn't?—you simply must learn to live by these five laws and never break them. These laws of money are timeless truths that will guide you to make sure you get exactly to where you want to go. They work no matter how old you are or where you stand with your money right now, whether we are in a bull or bear market, or whether the economy is up or down. These laws are your guide to true financial well-being.

Here are a few of the things you will learn in this book:

- How always telling the truth increases the flow of money into your life.

- Why actions based on fear will never make you rich.

- Why keeping company with people who break the laws of money will cause you to lose your money, too.

- How to improve your credit scores so you can get the lowest interest rates on credit cards, mortgages, and car loans.

- How to make sure you will never lose your home, car, or ability to pay your known expenses.

WHERE DO THESE LAWS COME FROM?

The five laws in this book actually come from you, from my dealings with tens of thousands of people over twenty-three years, and from my realization that those who are in financial trouble all got there exactly the same way—by breaking these five laws.

If you adhere to the essential laws contained in this book, the lessons you learn from your money will be life-affirming. After all, money's laws are not here to restrict you. They are here simply to keep you out of trouble, to make sure you are safe, to keep you from causing financial harm to yourself or others, and to bring you profound financial, emotional, and spiritual rewards. With the laws as your guides, you will be more, have more, and create more. That's the sequence. You can do this. It's not an empty promise. It's a law.

THE
LAWS *of*
MONEY

Law Number *1*

TRUTH CREATES MONEY, LIES DESTROY IT

*T*his is the most basic of all the laws. It stems from the universal moral code against lying or bearing "false witness," as the Ninth Commandment states. It's also the easiest law to see in action. In fact, we see it working around us every day. Unfortunately, we often see it working in its negative form (when lies destroy money), as in cases where the lies by executives in corporations cause stock values to plummet, companies to implode, and jobs and investments to be lost. The stories in which truth creates money are often less flashy than the newsworthy negative ones, but they do occur—and no doubt they are occurring in your life right now—even if they don't make the nightly news.

As a first step to understanding this law, think about how you present yourself to the world. People can tell a lot about you from a first impression. They see your smile, teeth, eyes, hair, if your nails are cared for, how you walk and speak. From these clues, they gauge any number of things about you. Right or wrong, these first impressions are indelible.

Along with this important first personal impression you make to the world, you also make a first financial impression. The funny thing, however, is that it is far easier to make a false first financial impression than a false first personal impression. If you are shy, it will be difficult, no matter how hard you try, to create the impression that you are outgoing, confident, and full of self-assurance. Yet financially, you can easily create the impression—the false impression—that you have more (or less) than you do.

Imagine this:

Two moms pull up to a school, one behind the other, to drop off their children. The first mom is driving a ten-year-old economy sedan. When she climbs out of this car, she is wearing neat but not very fashionable office clothes, and her child is dressed in practical clothes. The second mom drives up. Her car is shiny and seemingly very expensive, a brand new car that still has that new-car look. People can't help but notice this automobile, for it's the kind that most people would long to own, if they could only figure out how to afford it. When the second mother gets out, she's wearing a designer-label suit; her child has the latest brand-name clothes and a backpack that all the kids envy.

Picture these two people for a moment. What is your first impression of each of them, financially speaking? If you had to give a quick answer, you would probably say that the first mom does not have very much money and that the second mom has a lot. But what if I told you that the first mom can easily afford an even better and more expensive car than the second mom is driving, but would rather wait until her old car, which she paid for long ago, wears out? What if I told you that she earns more at her job than the second mom does, by a lot? What if I told you that she has a good, diversified retirement plan in place that has far more money in it than most people her age, and that she is already saving systematically for her child's college education? And what if I told you, too, that the second mom, the one with the shiny new car, is leasing the car, and that she truly cannot afford even to lease it, much less own it? And that she has no savings, no retirement plan, and $15,000 worth of credit card debt? And that she has serious doubts that she will ever be able to help her child pay for college? And that her biggest fear in life is that she will one day end up on the street as a bag lady, powerless and penniless?

You tell the world every day, in minor and profound ways, who you are, financially speaking. You express this through the clothes you wear, the car you drive, the house you live in, the shopping bags you carry, and dozens of other outward subtle cues. But are you telling the truth? More important, every day you also tell *yourself* who you are, by the choices you make with your money and the effect these choices have on your life and future. Again, how truthful are you to yourself?

When lies are woven into the fabric of your financial life, that fabric will inevitably fray.

Over the years I have come to learn that, to one extent or another, most people tend to lie about who they are when it comes to their money. I have learned the hard way that financial lies destroy financial lives, and that telling the truth about yourself and your money is the only way to keep what you have and create what you deserve.

SUZE'S LESSON

LYING TO MYSELF ALMOST DESTROYED ME

After leaving college, in 1973, I worked for seven years as a waitress at the Buttercup Bakery in Berkeley, California. From there—as the result of a fluke set of circumstances—I became a stockbroker trainee at Merrill Lynch. When I arrived at this job I knew how to make a great cheese omelet, but I knew nothing about money and nothing about stocks. So why did they hire me? Well, I do not know for sure, although I have always suspected that in 1980 big companies like Merrill Lynch were feeling pressure to hire women. I will never forget that, when I was hired, the office manager told me that women belonged barefoot and pregnant. He predicted I would be out of there in just six months. That did not deter me; I was thrilled to have this job.

I learned the trade very well, began to make money, and three years later was lured away by an offer I could not refuse: to become a vice president–investments for Prudential Bache Securities.

From the moment I became a stockbroker, I loved the money I was making. It was the first real money I had ever known. My greatest joy was to send copies of my checks to my mom, who could not believe that I was making $3,000 to $10,000 a month. I began to meet more sophisticated people, and it was fun to buy nice clothes and eat regularly in the kinds of restaurants I had been to before only as a rare treat. It was fun to earn that kind of money, and it was fun to spend it. It was as if the money I could now spend was a badge of my success.

After a time at Prudential Bache, I realized that my clients needed more from a financial advisor than just someone who would buy and sell stocks, bonds, and mutual funds for them. I wanted to serve them a full plate of financial choices, just as I had once wanted to serve my customers at the Buttercup Bakery not only a side of two eggs over easy but a full meal—say, a cheese omelet made with three different cheeses, onions, tomatoes, and peppers, and topped off with toast and jam, hash browns (with sour cream and chives), crispy bacon, and a fresh cup of coffee. I wanted to help my clients piece together all the parts of their financial lives. To do so I became a Certified Financial Planner® professional while still working for Prudential Bache, and started to apply everything I learned about what people really needed to do to protect their money and create more money for themselves. In order to best serve them and myself, I decided to open up my own firm, which I did in 1987.

In its very first few weeks my business just took off. In a short time, I was earning more money than ever before. For a while, with my checkbook leading the way, I became one of the happiest people I knew.

But my happiness didn't last. Soon after my firm was established, I was nearly destroyed by one of the most devastating things that ever happened to me—or so it seemed at the time. I know now, though, that what happened was a blessing, for it taught me one of the most important lessons of my life.

To this day, what happened remains vivid to me. An assistant who had worked for me at one of my previous jobs, a woman who I had brought with me to help me start my firm, sneaked into the office at 1:30 A.M. and made copies of all my client files and other records. The next day, she started making accusations about me that were utterly untrue, and, in my opinion, were meant to try to destroy me so that she could take over all my clients. I still don't know exactly why she did this, but I'm sure that, as is often the case in life, I must have seriously, although unknowingly, done something that caused her to hate me enough to lead her to act the way she did. At the time, however, I was heartbroken and angry, and I wanted revenge. The thing that confused me most was that I had no understanding of how someone I'd brought into my life voluntarily and wanted to help could want to hurt me in this way. But that story is about someone else's lies. This story is about my own.

There was an investigation, in the course of which it was discovered that I had not filed certain paperwork correctly, documents I needed in order to have my licenses in place. I basically was given a wrist slap and exonerated very quickly. Nonetheless, the legal victory did not help to heal my heart. During the investigation and even afterward, I just did not feel up to seeing my clients again. I put my business on hold. Still, instead of living as cautiously and frugally as I could, I continued to spend money like it was going out of style. Now that I look back, it seems curious that, even though I knew I should steer the course I would have advised my clients to take when their financial lives were threatened, I did not do so.

Instead, I chose to continue to live what I now see as a financial cover-up. I told almost no one what was truly going on in my life. For all my inner turmoil, outwardly I made light of my situation, behaving as if I had not a care—financial or otherwise—in the world.

The more depressed I became, the more I spent. After months of not earning and yet spending as though money were still rolling in, it did not take me long to go through all my savings. I began to rack up serious credit card debt, which was easy to do, since by then I had built up a large line of credit that I had not previously taken advantage of. Every month my credit card bills were huge, and were getting huger. I could barely afford to make the minimum payments on them all. I would go out to dinner with a group of friends, for example, and insist on paying the check. I wanted to keep up my image with others, as well as with myself, as a successful financial advisor. I was afraid that people would not like me or want to be around me if I did not have money. For I then believed that people liked me for what I had and not for who I was.

At this time I was also romantically involved with someone

who had a serious sum of money, and I lied to that person as well. I paid for an expensive trip to Mexico for the two of us, kept exchanging extravagant gifts that I could not afford, and had conversations full of lies about all the money I was making. Before long, I was tapping into my retirement accounts—no matter that I had to pay taxes, as well as penalties, on the money—just so that I could go on living this lie of appearing to have more money than I did. Meanwhile, everything I actually did have was quickly disappearing.

One day when I was driving over the Bay Bridge from San Francisco to Oakland, my whole world of lies came tumbling down around me. What happened was simple and small compared to everything else that was going on, yet it was the straw that broke the camel's back: I got a speeding ticket. I remember that the ticket was for only $40. But I did not have $40—I didn't have $20, or even $10, unless I was to take another cash advance on one of my credit cards. As I drove away from the bridge in my high-end leased car, wearing my $8,000 credit-card-charged watch and my $2,000 department-store-charged leather jacket, the magnitude of my lies became real to me for the first time. I was speeding down the highway to financial ruin.

When I got home that day, the truth started to pour out of me in the form of uncontrollable tears. I could not stop crying. Then I remembered something a wise teacher had once told me: Tears are God's way of forgiving you. I realized that the only way I could forgive myself was to start to tell the truth right then and there. And as the words were flowing out of me, the most important listener was me. I needed to say it. I needed to hear it. I needed to start living it. For even though I had been lying to the world, the person I had been destroying was me.

THE TRUTH IS NOT JUST A FACT, IT IS A PATH

It was amazing what happened when I began to live the truth. I stopped having the desire to give a false financial impression to others and started to show people who I really was. As soon as I did this, I started to feel better about myself. I began to feel more powerful, and when I felt more powerful, I had more energy. When I had more energy, I was able to make more of an effort to create what I wanted, which was to get beyond the hurt of what had happened and to get on with my life and my business.

If I hadn't had that experience on the bridge, I might have been financially devastated. But I learned a life lesson that was even more valuable and enduring than just how to survive rough financial times. I came to understand something very basic about the nature of truth and lies. I learned that the truth does not change, no matter how much you wish it would or what you do to obscure it. I learned that the truth is not so much a fact as a path, a path that leads to abundance of all kinds only when you choose to walk along it and stay within its course.

For the first time, I also saw that a lie is more than just an excuse to avoid doing something you know you need to do. A lie is also more than an excuse for actually doing something that you know will hurt you or someone else. A lie actively covers up the truth and robs you of your power. It forms the first link in a chain of events that will lead you away from control over your money and control over your life. In this sense, a lie is also a path, one that leads to destruction.

From that time on, I have been on the lookout for how the financial predicaments of the people who write, call, phone, and email me for advice have actually started with a simple lie. Here is what I have discovered from my many thousands of observations: When it comes to your money, almost every hour of every day presents a choice about whether to tell a lie or tell the truth.

For example, when your sister asks for a loan you don't want to give her, will you tell her you can't afford it, or will you tell her that, even though you can afford it, you are choosing not to give it to her? Or, when all your friends are going on vacation and ask you to come along but you don't have the money, will you lie and tell them that there is no way your boss will give you the time off (even though you are owed three weeks of vacation and that would be the perfect time to take it) or will you tell the truth, explaining that you currently have credit card debt and don't have the money to go on vacation?

Each decision you make with your money puts you at a crossroads between truth and lies. One road leads to creating what you want, the other to destroying what you have.

THE LEVELS AND LAYERS OF LIES

In varying layers and levels, most people lie about money. Do you exaggerate what you have, in order to exaggerate who you are? If so, I am here to tell you that this exaggeration can lead to the destruction of your own wealth as well as that of your associates and loved ones.

Always remember that, no matter how good any financial situation may look at the moment, if it is not grounded in the truth, the foundation it has been built upon will eventually crumble. Lies destroy money, and truth creates it. Why is this? It's because lies destroy trust, and the loss of trust results in the loss of power. And when you are powerless, you make the wrong decisions with your money.

I am asking you to remember—always—the corporate scandals at Enron, WorldCom, Tyco, and Arthur Andersen, the mutual fund industry, and the New York Stock Exchange. Think of those chief executive officers, chief financial officers, and those in charge of the guilty mutual funds. Their lies propelled them to huge wealth. For a while, they were the envy of their peers: rich, powerful, masters of their own financial fate—or so it seemed. Even you envied them. Isn't it true that you would read about their success or drive by the mansions owned by the many people who had great wealth, thinking, "Wow, if only I could live in a house like that"? Or, "Wow, if only I could have their kind of money"? Yet think about what happened when their lies finally emerged. They were utterly destroyed emotionally and financially. And the house that many of them most likely will reside in has no key, contains only four walls, and is known as jail. Now, the same people whom you envied are held in contempt by those they wished to impress.

It is important to recognize that all of these people once stood at a crossroads, where they had to make a choice about whether to take the path of a lie or the path of the truth. Do you think that if they could turn back the hands of time they might possibly—just maybe—choose the path of truth? Theirs are grand-scale morality tales, but the actions they took created the consequences that followed. This is true in all our lives, regardless of how large or small our actions or our fortunes are. If you lie about who you are with your money, you will tend to spend more than you have, buy a house without knowing whether you can afford it, act on impulse rather than rational knowledge, and take tragic actions with your own money that could easily destroy your own financial life.

YOUR LIES

I want you to trace the history of a current financial situation that you do not like and want to change. Perhaps you are standing on a mountain of debt that you are afraid will topple you. Perhaps you're in a relationship that makes you miserable but are afraid to leave because you are worried about money. Perhaps you feel you cannot find a job that will pay you enough to live. Perhaps you lent a friend $5,000 four years ago to help her when she had a heart attack and to this day she has not repaid you one penny and you do not have the nerve to say anything to her. Or perhaps you are angry at your spouse, partner, or yourself because at the start of the new millennium you had $100,000 in your 401(k) plan and now you have only $30,000; you wanted to sell your stocks and mutual funds but others told you, or you told yourself, that it would be okay if you just held on, and now you wish you had taken action.

Whatever your situation is, think about it as truthfully as you can.

Next, I want you to ask yourself why this happened to you. Walk yourself mentally backward, step by step, right to the beginning of the situation. In the back of this book is a guidebook that will help you go through this exercise in detail. Please heed this note of caution: As you do this exercise, you are not to blame others for your situation. I want you to see how it was you and no one else who created the situation you are in. This is usually the hardest part of the exercise, because we all tend to want to blame others for an uncomfortable situation we happen to be experiencing. It is human to think, "I have debt because my sister or my friend did not pay me back." "I have no money to retire because my financial advisor lost it all for me." "I once had all my money invested in Enron or WorldCom; now I have nothing left because the people who ran the company were crooks."

At the time of the events in my story, I blamed my financial demise on my assistant. But she was not really to blame. It was what I did to myself, not what she did to me, that caused my financial devastation, and it all started with a lie. You see, I knew, after working with this woman prior to starting my own business, that I did not really like or trust her. But I was afraid to tell her the truth about what I really thought of her, so I continued to lie to myself about who she was, continued to lie to her about my wanting to support her, and continued to lie to my clients about how great she was—all because I did not have the courage to tell the truth. I brought her with me because it was easier to do so than to tell her the truth about why I did not want to have her around me. Do you see what happened as a consequence? Do you see how I did this to myself? It started with a lie. If I had simply told her the truth, who knows what direction my life might have taken.

What lie have you told yourself that created the financial situation that you are currently in and want to change? What lie has rendered you powerless and sucked up your financial energy and therefore your money? Please think about these questions and note any insights you have in the guidebook.

All destruction starts with a lie, personal or financial.

PATRICK'S LESSON

TRYING TO LOOK GOOD TO OTHERS DESTROYS THE GOOD YOU HAVE

The Path of the Lie

"I wish they would just stop calling me. Every time the phone rings, I'm afraid to answer, because I know it's a debt collector trying to get money from me. Right now, I have $33,000 in credit card debt and I'm unemployed, and I don't have the money to send in even the minimum payments on my cards. I wish I did!"

How did Patrick get into this situation? What lie did he tell to himself and how would the truth have changed the situation? Let's trace the steps.

Patrick's story starts about a year and a half ago. One day, while he was at the office where he worked as a designer—full-time but on a freelance basis—his best friend from college called. "Guess what?" the buddy said. "Brad, Joe, Arthur, and I and the rest of our old fraternity gang are signing up to go on a three-week river-rafting trip in South America. The trip is next September. It costs five thousand dollars each, including airfare, but we only have to put down one thousand now. We can pay the rest before we go. It will be awesome. Want to come?"

Patrick hesitated. He didn't have $1,000, let alone $5,000, and he had been hearing that freelancers at his company were going to be laid off. He knew he shouldn't risk it. On the other hand, he had five credit cards, one of them brand-new; none had any charges on them, and together they gave him a credit limit of $33,000. He didn't want to miss a trip with the guys, and he sure didn't want to tell his friends that he couldn't afford to go, for in his eyes they were all doing so much better than he was. He said he'd go and charged the $1,000 to one of his cards. He told himself he'd save up the extra money he needed by September.

Flash-forward three months. Patrick and the other freelancers at his company have been laid off. Having had the time and discipline to save only $800 of the money he needs for the trip, he is now using those funds to meet his current expenses, supplementing the small checks he is getting for the few freelance projects he's been able to find.

When September rolls around, Patrick is afraid to tell his friends the truth, so he charges the additional $4,000 for the trip and heads off to South America for three weeks with his buddies. He talks himself into feeling okay about it, telling himself that he deserves a vacation—even though he knows that what he really wants and needs to be doing is looking for work and not spending money he does not have.

As soon as Patrick returns home, his physical and financial worlds are turned upside down. While he was gone, a torrential rainstorm came through his town, and a small leak in his roof, which Patrick had known about but had not gotten around to fixing, proved to be his greatest nightmare. He walks into his home to find that the ceiling, walls, carpeting, and furnishings in his bedroom have been destroyed. He gets in his car to drive to the hardware store for plastic to cover the ceiling, but the car will not start; it hasn't been driven in three weeks, and the battery, which was old to begin with, is now completely dead. The next day, he learns that his insurance company won't pay to repair the roof or structural damage and will pay only part of the cost of replacing his furniture.

Cost to Patrick: $5,000 to fix the roof, $1,500 for repairs to the walls and ceiling, $300 for cleanup supplies, $1,500 for a new bed, dresser, carpet, and TV, and $150 for a new car battery. Plus: $5,000 for his rafting vacation, $400 for additional meals he charged, and $200 for clothes and equipment he bought before he left on his trip. Total: $14,050 in credit card debt.

But the damage does not stop here. All Patrick's freelance work dries up, so no money whatsoever is coming in.

Patrick has to take cash advances from his credit cards just to pay for his mortgage, food, and gasoline—as well as to make payments on the previous balances on his cards. Here he is now, just about a half a year after he got back from what, in his mind, was a well-deserved vacation, and he has $33,000 in credit card debt. He has maxed his cards to the limit and cannot afford to make even the minimum payments on any of them. He has no idea what to do.

The real tragedy, however, is that while on vacation Patrick missed a call from his boss at his old company asking him to come back to work. When he returned his boss's call, he was heartbroken to learn that this boss, who wanted Patrick to work for him more than anyone else, had thought when Patrick did not return the call promptly that he had found himself another job. The company had decided to add just one full-time job to its roster, so the call Patrick missed would have given him a permanent staff position.

With no work and no way to pay his credit card bills, the calls from creditors begin.

Where did Patrick's troubles start? They started when he lied to himself and his best buddy by saying that it was okay to take a trip he knew he couldn't afford.

THE PATH OF THE TRUTH

Let's see what might have happened if Patrick had chosen the path of the truth rather than the path of the lie.

The story starts about a year and a half ago. One day, while Patrick was at the office where he worked as a freelance designer, his best friend from college called. "Guess what?" the buddy said.

"Brad, Joe, Arthur, and I and the rest of our old fraternity gang are signing up to go on a three-week river-rafting trip in South America. The trip is next September, ten months from now. It costs $5,000 each, including airfare, but we only have to put down $1,000 now. We can pay the rest before we go. Want to come?"

Patrick hesitated. He didn't have $1,000, let alone $5,000, and he had been hearing that freelancers at this company were going to be laid off. He knew he shouldn't risk it. So he said to his college buddy, "Hey, I'd give my right arm to go on this rafting trip with you guys, but I don't have the money right now. Make sure you take some great pictures for me."

If Patrick had taken this path, he would not have charged $5,600 for the trip ($5,000, plus $400 in meals and $200 in clothing and equipment).

He would have been at home when the news was broadcast that a brutal storm was on its way. When he heard the news, he could have acted to get his roof fixed, or at least patched, in time to save his bedroom ceiling, walls, and furniture. Eventually, he would still have needed to spend $5,000 to fix his roof, and that $5,000 would have gone on his credit cards, but he would not be out of pocket all the money he spent to clean up the mess and replace his furniture. His car battery would not have died, because he would have been driving the car the whole time and the battery would have remained charged. And the biggest change that would have taken place in Patrick's financial future, of course, is that he would have been home to get the call from his old boss. He would be back at work full-time, earning more than ever, and able to make payments on the $5,000 he put on his credit card to fix the roof. And all would be just fine.

Patrick's lie led to financial destruction. The truth would have led to financial creation. It happens every day.

Now, think again about your own situation, the one I asked

you to trace back. How is your situation based on a lie, conscious or unconscious? At the same time, I want you to think about what the truth really is in your situation, and how, if you had just acted from the truth, your situation would be different right now.

Here are some examples. You can read through these and make notes to yourself in the guidebook as you remember your own situation.

If you are facing serious debt, did you lie by telling yourself that you would soon get a raise at work and be able to pay off your debt, knowing all the while that, in truth, the more money you made the more you spent? As you look back over the years, is it true that even as you made more money you also had more debt?

If you are afraid to leave a bad relationship, are you telling yourself that you cannot take care of yourself on your own, when the truth is that you have been taking care of yourself and the person with whom you are in the relationship from day one?

If others owe you money and have not paid you back, what is the lie that started this off? Did you say, "Okay, I will lend you the money and I feel great about it," when the truth was "I do not want to lend you money; I can't afford it and it just doesn't feel right"?

If you have lost money in the stock market, was the lie that you kept telling yourself that you did not have to watch over your money because someone else was doing it for you? Or that you did not need to diversify a portfolio made up entirely of technology stocks? Or that your stocks or mutual funds were immune to the decline that the rest of the market suffered? Or that your stocks would surely bounce back over time, and that therefore you did not have to pay attention to them?

The truth is that of course you must keep watch over your money, for what happens to your money directly affects the quality of your life—not your financial advisor's life, not your banker's life, not my life. Of course you must diversify your holdings, for that is one of the basic truths about investing. Of course you cannot blindly believe that your stocks are exempt from the general direction of the market, for as you now may know, that is not true.

I am sure that one of the hardest aspects of this law will be for you to accept the role that you yourself have had in any serious investment losses you experienced as the stock market plummeted in the first few years of the new century; you may even have lost 50 percent of your money. But I ask you right here and now to address this situation in the exercise above. Ask yourself who forced you to stay invested. Why did you not sell some of your stocks or mutual fund holdings as they declined in value? Did you listen to yourself or did you hand over your power to a financial advisor, who was probably telling you that he knew what he was doing but actually may not have had a clue himself? (Later, I'll want you to do this in the guidebook in detail.)

The truth is it is impossible for any financial advisor to know what the market will or will not do. Even with the gains in the market that started in spring 2003, your portfolio may still be down. For instance, at the start of 2004, the NASDAQ is up 77 percent from its low in October 2002, but it is still down 61 percent from its high of March 2000. So, for the NASDAQ just to break even from these numbers, it would take ten years at a 9 percent annual average rate of return. Nonetheless, some so-called financial experts do not know the laws of money and some simply ignore them. I only wish that I could turn back the clock for you, so that you would not have to suffer the losses that you experienced. But I cannot. All I can do is help you learn from what happened in the past few years and help you try to make sure that it never happens again.

Which leads me to another important point about truth and lies: It is not only the lies that you tell yourself that will affect your money. The lies that other people tell you will also affect your money. Another person's truth will become a lie for you, if it is not the truth for your life. Even unintentional lies, such as sales pitches, lies that others attempt to get you to believe, can have a devastating impact.

Here's what you have to understand: Many of the people from whom you are getting your financial information—analysts on TV, financial advisors, personal bankers, and insurance agents—do not really know what is best for you. They may believe what they are telling you is true, but if it is not true for you, it is as good as a lie.

Some of these people may not even have your best interests at heart. They may be thinking about their own best interests, about making a sale or a commission. If that is the case, then they may tell you what they think you want to hear, or what will convince you to let them continue to do what they have been hired to do: first and foremost, to make money for their firms; secondly, to make money for themselves; and only then, if all goes well, to make money for you. The recommendations they make on investments are sometimes truly the best investments, but sometimes are among the biggest financial mistakes that you could make.

Please do not misunderstand me. Many—probably most—financial advisors are really good people. (Remember, I used to be one, and in my own way, I still am.) Many advisors innocently sell you investments, having themselves believed the sales pitches their firms supply to them. But in a strange way, you choose whether to believe what other people are telling you or to believe what you yourself deeply feel and know. And you usually know when someone is not giving you the information that is best for you. When you don't act on that knowledge, it is often because you do not trust your own truth enough to tell the other person that you don't want to act on his or her advice—and then you lose. We'll see more about this with Law 2.

ACTING FROM A PLACE OF TRUTH

It is one thing to read Law 1 and it is another thing to live it. The question you now have to answer is: How do you act from a place of truth from this day on, so that you do not continue to sabotage your financial life with lies? Earlier you did an exercise where you identified a financial situation that you would like to change. You traced the roots of that situation back to a lie and explored how it would have been different if you had acted from the truth. Now you have to put that truth into action, because it is not enough just to know the truth—you have to become the truth.

I have a favorite saying that helps me gain the courage to change direction whenever I start to take an inappropriate course: If you are heading the wrong way, remember that God permits U-turns. When I first heard these words, I thought, "That's great, but I'm not sure how to do that." Then I got it, and so can you. You see, even though God permits U-turns, it is you and only you who can act to change the course of your financial vehicle. You must grab hold of that steering wheel, turn it, and drive yourself in the right financial direction.

So how do we make that U-turn? The first and most essential step is to forgive yourself for any lies you told or mistakes you made. Just as I don't want you to blame others for your situation, I do not want you to blame yourself either. Taking responsibility and blaming yourself are not the same thing.

When you look at what you did to get to this point, it is so that you can learn your life lesson and move on from there. Guilt and blame are of no help in moving forward.

Changing direction also involves making that U-turn and actually going back over every inch of the bumpy financial road you've followed. As you review where you've been, you need to stop at every point along the way where you have told a financial lie. When you arrive at one of these points, you have to make an effort—no matter what it takes—to correct your lie. You have to face what got you to where you are right now. This is not easy, but it must be done.

Think of the friend to whom you lent money and who has still not paid you back. You must set the record straight by telling her, over the phone or in a letter, how you felt when you made the loan, exactly how you feel now, and what action you want to take to close that chapter of your financial life.

Think about the credit card collectors you've been avoiding, or even lying to by telling them when they call that no one by your name lives there. You must call them, tell them the truth, and deal with your situation head-on.

Think about the friends who keep asking you to go out to dinner, to the movies, or to a ball game—and do not have a clue that you have $15,000 of credit card debt. You must tell them the truth about the amount of credit card debt you have, and explain that it is not respectful to yourself or your future—or to them—to keep going out and spending money you don't have.

Think of your financial advisor, the one you no longer trust or feel comfortable with. You must tell him why you feel this way and then take the necessary actions to learn how to manage your own money or to find someone you can trust to work with.

The greatest truth that I want you to remember, however, is this: Other people's feelings do not determine your value in life.

If you lie to spare people's feelings, to make a strong first financial impression, or, as in my own story, because you are not sure
who you are without the trappings of success, it is important to
know—from this moment forward—that you are perfect just
the way you are. I mean this with all my heart. It is what I discovered by facing the truth in my own life. And I discovered
something more: Keeping what you have and creating what
you deserve is not only about money. It is about the absence of
fear, which is an even greater blessing than the absence of want;
and fear tends to disappear when you tell the truth. It is about
liking who you are and sleeping well at night. It is about recognizing that you and your money are one; when you know this,
then the actions you take with your money and the actions you
take with your life will be one and the same, and the ways in
which you behave with your money will reflect the truth about
who you are.

It all starts with deciding to lie or tell the truth. It's up to you.

THE LESSONS FROM LAW 1:
TRUTH CREATES MONEY, LIES DESTROY IT

- Every day you tell yourself who you are, financially and in
  other important ways, by the choices you make with your
  money.
- When lies are woven into the fabric of your financial life,
  that fabric will inevitably fray.
- The truth does not change, no matter how much you wish it
  would or what you do to obscure it.
- Do not be afraid that people will not like you or want to be
  around you if you do not have money. Good people everywhere will like you for who you are, not for what you have.

+ Be careful not to let the money you spend become a badge of your success.

+ The person who most needs to hear and tell the truth about your money is you. You need to speak the truth. You need to hear the truth. And you need to start living the truth.

+ The truth is not so much a fact as a path, a path that leads to abundance of all kinds only when you give it a voice—your voice—and then act on it.

+ A lie actively covers up the truth and robs you of your power. It forms the first link in a chain of events that will lead you away from control over your money and control over your life.

+ Every hour of every day presents a choice about whether to tell a lie or tell the truth when it comes to your money. The choice is up to you.

+ Each decision you make with your money puts you at a crossroads between truth and lies. One road leads to creating what you want, the other to destroying what you have.

+ Keeping what you have and creating what you deserve is not only about money. It is about the absence of fear, which is even a greater blessing than the absence of want.

+ Financial lies destroy financial lives. Telling the truth about yourself and your money is the only way to keep what you have and create what you deserve.

+ It is important to know that you are perfect just the way you are.

Law Number 2

LOOK AT WHAT YOU HAVE, NOT AT WHAT YOU HAD

*N*ow that you've begun to examine how your financial life has evolved as a consequence of the truths and lies you've told, I want you to stop and look around you, wherever you are. Please take a deep breath. Now, take a truthful, fearless look at who you are and what you really have in your life.

If you are like most people, you will have to take stock of where you are financially after living through a roller-coaster ride of economic and world changes. And what may keep you from getting a clear reading of your situation and formulating a good action plan for your money is the cloud of disappointment, anger, or fear hanging over your memories about whatever setbacks you've already been through. It's time to tell the truth about where you are right now, today, so that you can move forward competently and confidently into your financial future.

The principle behind this law ties in to the Tenth Commandment, about not "coveting" anyone else's belongings or relationships, life situation, or talents. Nor are you supposed to long for something that is past, over and done with, gone. That is a terrible waste of your energy, time, and money, and no good can come of it. Let yourself see the truth about what you really have right now.

LIVING IN THE PAST WILL NOT CREATE A FUTURE

Have you ever known someone who lost the love of his life? Maybe his fiancée left him for someone else, or his parents insisted that he go to college instead of getting married. In such cases, it sometimes happens that this person lives his life always thinking, "If only . . ." "If only I had married Carmen, I'd be happy." "If only Carmen were here with me, I'd have the courage to do anything." "If only I were good enough for Carmen, I'd be better off." However much you sympathize with this person over his sadness, sooner or later his obsession with the past will begin to irritate you. Why can't he look at what he has, or at least take a look around? If he did, you think, he might notice that two great possible catches, Kathy and Mary, are standing right in front of him and seem to be trying to catch his eye.

But this is not how most people operate. We hang on to the past, allowing it to define who we are today.

It's the same with our money. Many people have suffered financial losses at some time in their lives. Those losses may stem from expenses related to a medical condition that insurance did not cover, a divorce or separation, a job loss, or investments that have plummeted in value, or simply from being irresponsible with money. Sometimes we react to such

losses by regaining our balance, doing what's right for ourselves and for the money we still have, and moving on. Other
times, we keep waiting for the world to change back again
and make our financial situation right. When that happens,
we are living in the past. Sometimes this means spending
money we no longer have. Sometimes it means giving up and
doing nothing. Often, it means fooling ourselves into believ-
ing that, if we just keep going the way we're going, things will
magically turn out all right. For many people, it has meant
that, if you just keep holding on to the stocks and mutual
funds that you had originally bought in the 1990s, one day
they will come back to what they were worth at the start of
the year 2000.

In hundreds of circumstances and dozens of ways, people
hang on to the past and cause the destruction of their future. By
making this one mistake—simply looking back at what you had
instead of looking at what you have right now, and deciding
what you are going to do with it—you could ultimately lose
much of what you have.

Please note that although this law is about financial losses,
it is also about who you were and who you are, and it applies
to every aspect of your life. When you hang on to the past, you
affect how you feel about yourself in many of the situations you
currently find yourself in, wherever you are in your life.

We all reflect on past experiences, of course—and when we
do so in a way that serves our best interests, this helps us. Looking back is the way we learn from our mistakes and pat ourselves on the back for the good things we've done. But living in
the past is another story. There's nothing constructive about
habitually comparing your money to circumstances that no
longer exist. It simply leaves you stuck, ripe for getting into further trouble.

IT'S TIME TO WAKE UP TO WHO SHE IS

See if Lee's story reminds you of anyone you know or of how you have responded to situations in your own life.

I really can't understand myself. I'm a grown woman, I'm smart, I've had a career and earned money all my life, and yet I simply cannot bring myself to talk to my husband about money. I was forty-one when I married Walter, three years ago; I'd never been married before. Walter was fifty-one and had been married for twenty-two years (and divorced for five). He had—and has—a lot of money. I don't. And that's the crux of my problem.

I respect and admire Walter. He's a very old-fashioned kind of guy. He wears three-piece suits. He works hard. He made every dollar he has, by starting and running small computer companies. His father supported his mother, and Walter supported his first wife and children—still does; he once mentioned that he sends his ex-wife, who never worked, a lot of alimony, and that's after they divided everything equally between them at the time of the divorce. His twenty-five- and twenty-eight-year-old sons call and write for money. He sends it. Except for thinking that they might be better off learning to support themselves (like I did?), I don't mind.

You see, Walter supports me, too, although it might not look that way. I work, earn a respectable amount of money—and put most of that money in the bank. Meanwhile, he pays all the bills, buys our dinners in the

city's best restaurants, picks out and pays for the vacations we take, buys the furniture, even pays for many of
my clothes. When we go out to dinner with his friends
or my friends, unless someone grabs the check away
from him he pays. Sometimes he grabs it back. He's
incredibly generous and responsible. I never worry that
he's overspending. As far as I know, he's never been in
debt.

But I don't know how much money Walter makes, or
has, or where he keeps his money. We have no joint
accounts. I don't know what kind of insurance he has, or
what other financial obligations he is under. The apartment we moved into when we got married is in Walter's
name alone—partly, I think, because my credit rating
was terrible then. I had tax arrears; he paid them. When
we first moved into the apartment, I tried to get him to
let me pay a proportionate share of the mortgage and
maintenance, based on my income and my wild guess
about what his income might be; but every month, when
I'd give him a check, he'd hand it back to me. He wasn't
comfortable taking money from me, he said. And some
part of me was relieved, because giving Walter mortgage
money felt like paying rent. I don't own the apartment.
He does. And it's a little weird to be paying your husband
rent.

Until I met Walter, I lived on a shoestring and wasn't
exactly a beacon of financial responsibility, but I supported myself and never received a dime of help from
anybody. Now, financially speaking, I feel like a mistress
or a child. I'm being totally taken care of. The child in
me adores it, but even after three years, it all feels half-

real, as if it could go away at any moment, and what I'd be left with is what I had before: a struggle to pay rent every month on an apartment I didn't own, a big tax debt, monthly bills I hated to open, a faint, constant sense of bewilderment and envy of others' financial success, and a fear of financial insecurity that kept me working night and day at jobs I sometimes hated and was afraid to quit.

Today, I don't have that envy or that fear, but I think I must be afraid of looking at this new reality of mine too closely—for fear that it will turn out to be made of smoke and mirrors, or perhaps because I might have to insist on actually growing up and paying my rightful share. I know that Walter would talk to me about his money if I asked. I don't want to ask. I'm afraid. That's the size of it.

WHAT IS THE SOURCE OF LEE'S WORRIES?

Lee's story is fascinating because she is better off in every way than she used to be—but she still clings to her past. She's in a fortunate situation that many women would not be able to keep themselves from wishing they had. But she's not happy or secure. The problem is that Lee gives herself no credit whatsoever for the change in her financial situation or her life. She tells herself that, if she had not found Walter, she would still be in tax arrears, struggling to pay the rent, and living from hand to mouth. I don't think so. What I think is that while Walter may have helped her get started on a new financial path, he didn't rescue her. No one rescues us—except ourselves.

Let's look at Lee's current situation. Who keeps working for the money she earns? She does. Who saves it, instead of spending it on luxuries, as she could easily do? She does. Who is building a strong financial foundation for herself, in spite of what Walter has or doesn't have? She is—for since she and Walter are still essentially leading separate financial lives, Lee could easily lie about her money, but she does not. Just the same, she continues to hold on to the memories and emotions of a past in which she had less—and she half expects to go back to having less—because she still feels that she *is* less. The feeling is familiar to her.

The problem is not so much that Lee fears she will lose what she has or thinks she might not be able to create more; the problem is that she doesn't think more of herself. Deep down, she believes that she is still the same person who had to work at jobs she hated and was in trouble with the IRS.

WAKING UP TO THE NEW YOU

Many people are like Lee. Maybe you are too. You don't truly believe that you could have something or be something on your own. If you were poor once, or if you have experienced a failure in your life, or if you are in credit card debt or another kind of financial trouble now, you may not see that you can create—and may already have created—something better for yourself. So you live in dread of returning to the past; you carry the weight of the past with you wherever you go. But the truth is that you are what you do today, not what you did yesterday. To keep thinking otherwise is as misguided and wrong as my still thinking of myself as the person who earned $3.50 an hour at the Buttercup Bakery. Even if I found myself in that position again, do you think that I would do the same things I did then?

I would not, for I have changed. So has Lee. And so have you.

Law 2 says, in effect, that it is time to recognize who you have become, not dwell on who you were.

THROW OUT THE JEANS

To look at this law from another perspective, let's consider what you now have in your closet. Do you still have your old size 6 jeans, even though you are a size 14? If so, why? The answer is simple. It's not that you would not be able to afford another pair of size 6 jeans if you ever lost the weight you have gained, but that by throwing away the past, or the profile you had when you were a size 6, you would be forced to own up to the fact and live in the reality of what you do have now, which is a size 14 body. As it is, even though you know you are a size 14, you do not have to realize your gain, so to speak, as long as those old jeans are in the closet. Hanging on to the jeans allows you to hold on to what you were and what you had, and not embrace who you are and what you have now.

What good does this do you? If you are a size 14 and want to fit into size 6 jeans, holding on to the jeans does you no good at all. If only you could look at what you have to work with today, you might come to understand that what you had back then was very different. Then you were twenty-two. Today you are fifty. Then, no matter what you ate, you didn't gain weight. You never had to exercise, and still your body looked as if you ran four miles a day. Today, your metabolism moves at a snail's pace, and no matter what you eat you gain weight. You exercise a little bit, but it does not show. You feel as if all you have to do is look at a scale and another pound gets added. So you see, what you have today is very different from what you had back then.

The truth is that to become a size 6 you will need to change your eating habits and go to the gym a lot more often than once a month. You may even have go to a doctor for a checkup, to find out whether your heart, lungs, and other vital organs are functioning well enough for you to embark on a brand-new regimen. Staring at your old jeans and living in a fantasy world about how great you looked in them will not help you one bit in your quest to lose weight. In fact, it will harm you—because you will not have an accurate starting point for dealing with what is really going on or for taking the necessary actions to get you to where you want to be.

If you are clinging to an outdated view of yourself based on the past, it is imperative that you wake up, do a reality check, and see who you really are today and how to get from your new starting point to where you want to be tomorrow.

Remember, the past doesn't have any power over you—not unless you give it power. With Law 2, you are learning how the inability to accept loss, any loss of what you had, is what keeps you from moving on and recognizing the gains that you have already made—and can make. When you hold on mentally and emotionally to what you had, there is no way to create and recognize the greater wealth that you may already have. In Lee's case, that wealth includes a full understanding of how competent and responsible she is today.

THROW OUT THE PORTFOLIO

When it comes to your money, looking at what you have, not at what you had, is essential. Whether you have thousands in your own personal investment accounts, or just a few hundred dollars in your 401(k) or Roth IRA, many people are living in their financial past. As I travel the country, I constantly hear things like: "Suze, I had $300,000 in my 401(k) and now it is worth $120,000." Or "Suze, I had an investment portfolio worth $25,000 and now it has only $8,000 in it." Or "Suze, two years ago I had $1,400 in a mutual fund and now it has gone down to $80—when will it go back up to what I had?"

Isn't it true? Even though your portfolio started to come back in 2003, how many times a day do you think back to how much money you had at the start of the new millennium compared with how much you have today? Maybe you don't even know how much you have today—many people I talk to just don't even take the time to open their statements anymore. They don't even know what they have. This can be very, very dangerous.

SAM'S LESSON

NOT KNOWING WHEN TO LET GO CAN DESTROY YOU

I first met Sam, a TV cameraman, after I appeared on a network news show in January 2001. The minute the show was off the air, Sam came running up to me from behind his camera, saying in a hushed voice, "Suze, I have to talk to you. Please. Give me just a few minutes. I feel like I'm going crazy, and I'm desperate." He was pale, shaking, and sweating. He looked like he was withdrawing from drugs. But drugs were not Sam's problem. His problem was he was being drugged by his own financial acid trip—and was suffering flashbacks of what he had once had financially.

I'll never forget what Sam told me that evening—a story that had already cost him his life savings, his girlfriend, and his self-esteem, and was about to cost him his home and possibly his job. And yet, he told me, "I know it's going to turn around, Suze. I just have to figure out how to get through these next few weeks, and then everything will be okay again." When he said this, he looked like he was going to throw up. I knew he didn't believe it any more than I did.

Here's how, by unknowingly breaking Law Number 2, Sam nearly destroyed his financial life:

A few years ago a bunch of guys I worked with here at the TV studio began buying technology stocks, especially one particular stock by the name of Cisco. What I found so funny is that none of them even understood what Cisco really did, but that did not seem to matter to them. From September of 1998 to September of 1999, my friends tripled their money on that stock. They kept buying more of it, sometimes on credit or something that's called margin, and they kidded me, saying things like, "What's the matter, Sam, you scared of the market?"

In fact, I had never invested in the stock market. I had always saved my money in a money market fund and put everything I had into this house that I had purchased and just loved. It was a fabulous investment for me. Real estate in California was skyrocketing, but what I loved even more than the rising value was the appreciation I felt for the fact that this was my house and that I was working hard to own it outright. But to tell you the truth, even though I loved the way my house was going up in value, it was bugging me that if I had just invested with the guys in this one stock, I could have owned the house outright by now. The more they showed me how much money they were making, the more I regretted the fact that I did not buy in when they did. Finally, I thought, what the heck—what do I have to lose? And I decided to invest.

Most of my money was tied up in my home, so I decided that I would have to take out a home equity line of credit. I had the house appraised and found out that the fixer-upper I'd bought for $300,000 in 1991 and never really fixed up was by then, in October 1999, worth slightly over $900,000. I could not believe it. "Not bad!" I thought. This made me feel a little better about having missed out on the money I could have made in the stock market if I had just gone in with my friends two years earlier. I owed about $200,000 on the mortgage, so I could borrow about $500,000 from the house. I decided to take a $500,000 home equity line of credit, knowing that I still had a nice cushion remaining in my home, no matter what.

So I applied for the loan. This was in the beginning of November 1999, and Cisco was trading at about $36 a share. I thought I would quickly qualify for the loan—I had been working for many years as a cameraman at the same studio and made good money—but I had to clean up some questions on my credit report, so it took until mid-December to actually get the line of credit. By this time, I was sick to my stomach, because every day I was watching Cisco continue to climb, and every day I calculated how much money I would have made if I had only bought at $36. By the time the loan went through and I got the checkbook that would let me write a check for $500,000, Cisco was trading at $50 a share.

By this time, my friends all had far more than $500,000 invested in Cisco, and they said they thought I should wait until Y2K was over before I bought. Y2K was right around the corner, and no one knew what would happen. If nothing happened, they said, I could invest right after the new year. If something did happen, I would be glad that I had waited. They felt fine about staying in, since they'd bought Cisco when it was selling for only about $12 a share.

As each day passed and the stock continued to edge up, all I thought about was how much money I could already have made if only I'd had the line of credit and bought in November at $36 a share. But I knew I should be patient, so I waited to see what the new year would bring. Y2K passed with no problem, nothing, and on the very first day the market reopened I called the discount brokerage firm I had set up an account with and bought 9,000 shares of Cisco at around $54 a share.

The next few months were incredibly exciting, because every time Cisco went up by $1, I knew that I had made $9,000. I've never seen money like that. The guys at the studio were cheering me on, telling me that I would have to split the profits with them and that I owed them big time for making me so rich. And I have to tell you, I believed them.

Making money this way was addictive. Soon I wanted to make even more than I was making. I realized that I could do what the guys did by borrowing money against the equity in my brokerage account, which was now worth about $630,000, because in just four months Cisco had gone to $70 a share. I was told that I qualified to buy another 9,000 shares of Cisco. That would give me a total of 18,000 shares. Geez, all I could think about was the fact that if I had done that from the start, I would be up $288,000 right now instead of only $144,000. But that was okay. I knew I was about to make a whole lot more. So I went ahead and bought another 9,000 shares at $70. Now I owned 18,000 shares with an average cost basis of $62.50.

Sam, like so many other investors, had been seduced by the boom in the technology market, of which Cisco was a part. Knowing the history of Cisco pretty well, I wasn't surprised by Sam's seduction. Cisco was one of those incredible stock stories of the 1990s. It started out as a tiny little snoozer and climbed to dizzying heights, going from $8 a share in December 1997 to $80 a share in March 2000—the month that marked the exact top of the bull market in technology. That was about ten months before I met Sam. By April 2000, Cisco and all its high-flying cousins would begin to fall. But the stocks didn't drop in a straight line. For most of 2000 and 2001, those technology stocks would move down a little, then move back up a little. Then they would move down again. The general direction was south, but the up-and-down action caused millions of investors like Sam and his friends to hang on to what they had and kept them from dealing with what they currently did have, with disastrous consequences, as Sam relates in the next part of his story.

At the time, in early 2000, I still thought I was doing so great even though I had regrets over what I could have had if I just started out earlier. But I was loving the money I was now making. In the days after I had purchased 9,000 shares on margin at $70, Cisco continued to go up to $81 a share. I remember totaling up how much my stock was worth at that moment—about $1,450,000. I could not believe it. Along with the fair market value of my home, that made me a multimillionaire.

As the months went by, Cisco came off its high and started to go down, but it always kind of came back. The stock would go down into the 50s and come back into the high 60s—it just stayed in that range. It didn't bother me, because I knew it would go back up again, past 81. During this time, when it was going back and forth, I decided that when it did go back to 81 that I would sell it. As the year wore on, I refused to believe that Cisco was not coming back. But in December 2000—less than one year after I bought it—the stock was at $34 a share. And now I was in terrible trouble.

The terrible trouble that Sam was talking about is known as *margin calls*. Because Sam had borrowed money from his brokerage firm to buy more stock than he had money to pay for at the time—this is called *going on margin*—when his account fell below a certain value, the firm wanted Sam to repay the margin loan. It gave him a choice—come up with more money, or it would sell some of his stock. This way, the firm would be protected against losing the money it had lent him if the stock continued to go down in value.

When Sam first started to get margin calls, he wanted badly to hold on to his shares of Cisco until they went back up to where they had been, at $81. To do this, he raised cash to meet his margin calls by taking out even more equity from his house, which had continued to appreciate in value over the past year. When that equity was gone, he decided to take cash advances on his credit cards. When he'd tapped out his current cards, he went and took out what he could from his 401(k) plan as a loan. Meanwhile, he told me, he hadn't made either his mortgage or home equity loan payments for the past month. He had a pile of bills a mile high, and the creditors was sending him threatening notices.

Even in the face of all this debt, he did not want to let go of what, once upon a time, he had had on paper with Cisco. Having lost almost everything to keep what he thought he had, Sam was such a wreck that his job put him on warning, and his girlfriend, who hadn't approved of any of this brinkmanship financing, couldn't stand it anymore and left him. Looking at him that day— frantic, sweaty, scared, defiant, and still holding on to every share of his plummeting Cisco stock—I could understand why his girl- friend had done this. It would take something earthshaking to wake Sam up to the state of his money and the state of his life.

APRIL FOOL'S IS NOT A JOKE

I begged Sam to sell everything right then and there and told him what the probable consequences would be if he did not. He seemed to get it and said he would sell everything the next morn- ing. I called the next evening to see if he had done this. He had not. The problem was that earlier in the day, Alan Greenspan and the Federal Reserve Board had unexpectedly lowered the fed interest rate, and the market had started to take off. Cisco had moved up and closed that day at about $41 a share—and that gave Sam hope that all would go back to what he had. Sam told me that he had decided not to sell. No matter what I said to him, he did not want to listen.

Last time I heard from Sam, on April 1, 2001, Cisco was trading at $15 a share. He was still hanging on to the shares that the brokerage firm had not made him sell. Even if he's holding on to those shares today, at the start of 2004, they are only at $24 a share—still a considerable loss to Sam. He told me that he had just sold his home to help pay the bills and was about to move into a small apartment. One thing that gave me hope that maybe, just maybe, he was starting to get it, was when he asked me, "Do you think that they named this day after me?"

By the way, you might be wondering what happened to Sam's friends. All he would say when I asked was "What friends?"

THE FEAR OF LOSS CAUSES GREATER LOSS

Sam's example is extreme but instructive. He was so intent on looking back at what he once briefly had—on paper, at least—that he was paralyzed when it came to taking any steps at all to protect what he still did have in his life, including his home, his job, and his relationship with his girlfriend. The fear of loss causes greater losses. That's why denial of your present-day financial reality—your reality right now—is one of the biggest obstacles to financial wealth and emotional well-being.

You may not be as extreme as Sam—let's hope not! But are you really all that different from him?

Did you buy shares of a stock at $25 back in 1999—maybe in your IRA or 401(k)? Did you watch that stock go up to $50, then to $100, then to $150, and finally to $220? Why didn't you sell all or even some of your shares during this spectacular climb to $220? Probably because, like Sam, you were focused on a financial fantasy about what you would do with the money if the stock went all the way up to $275. And since you were distracted by a fantasy, you were not paying attention to the financial reality that you had already more than quadrupled your money. You were not thinking about the money you could have had right there, in the palm of your hand. You were filled with hope that you would have even more money if your stock continued to climb.

Then came the year 2000, and you watched your stock plunge back down to $150, then to $100, then to $75, and finally to $15. And as the stock fell, you kept thinking some of the things that Sam thought. "But I had $220 a share," you said. "I can't have lost all that money! The stock has to go back up, right?" Well, maybe yes. But remember that, as with Sam's case, even though it may go back up, you're still likely to sustain a significant, unrecoverable loss. This was the voice of your past speaking to you—it told you that if you sold, you would realize your losses and then they would be real. Remember the example of being a size 14 and holding on to your size 6 jeans? Do you understand that you must give those jeans away if you are to have an accurate starting point for a new beginning? Can you see how these examples are both the same?

DON'T FOOL YOURSELF

If Sam had been able to look at what he actually did have, he might have seen that his dreams for his life had already come true. If he had stayed focused on that, his situation would be a very different one today. Sam's situation would be different—and if you can personally relate to his story, so would yours.

Even if you bought into the stock market when it was at its all-time high and never really got to participate in the exhilaration of watching the market and your money go up and up, you still have to ask yourself the question, "Why didn't I sell as my money drained out of the stocks and mutual funds I owned and as I watched my balances go down?" The only answer is that, once again, you were focused on what you once had or could have had rather than what you did have at that moment.

REARVIEW MIRROR INVESTORS

Many people are what I call rearview mirror investors. Rearview mirror thinking applies to all kinds of financial decisions, but it applies most directly to investing. What Sam was doing was like driving home by looking in the rearview mirror. If you do this, you may make it for a few blocks without an accident, but sooner or later you will become a financial wreck. The purpose of investing is to help your financial life go forward from where you are. The easiest way to go forward is to look at where you are and at what you have, and then to decide where you want to go from here. You cannot go forward easily by looking back. Do you see why "Look at what you have, not at what you had" is a major law of money—one that you have to understand, accept, and use in your life?

WHAT SHOULD YOU DO NOW WITH WHAT YOU DO HAVE?

Of course, it is one thing to read this law and another thing to apply it to your life. Just as you had to learn how to see the truths and lies about money that exist all around you every day, you also have to learn how to see what your money is worth today. This can be especially challenging with respect to the stocks and mutual funds you currently own, either inside or outside of your retirement accounts.

YOUR EXERCISE

I want you to take out a piece of paper and duplicate the headings that are listed below. Or you can turn to the guidebook in the back of this book and complete the exercise there (page 225).

1. Name of Stock/ Mutual Fund/Real Estate/ Other Investment	2. Date of Purchase	3. Total Price Paid	4. Current Total Value	5. Gain or Loss	6. Would You Buy It Now?

1. In column 1, list every single stock or mutual fund or other investment you own, including real estate, variable annuities, variable life insurance, and whole life insurance.
2. In column 2, write down the date when you purchased this investment.
3. In column 3, fill in the total price that you paid, including all commissions. For instance, if you bought 1,000 shares of Cisco at $30 and you paid $47 in commissions, write $30,047 in column 3.
4. In column 4, fill in the total value of what that investment is worth today.
5. In column 5, write the amount you get by subtracting the total price you paid in column 3 from the total value in column 4. That is your gain. If the amount is a loss, enclose it in parentheses.
6. For every investment that you currently own, ask yourself, if you did not own it today and you had the amount of money in column 4 in cash, would you buy it right now—buy this stock, mutual fund, or other investment? Write down your answer—yes, no, or don't know—in column 6.

LET'S PLAY BALL—KEEP OR SELL

Look at column 6 in your chart. For every time you answered no, you would not buy this investment right now if you had the cash to do so, look into selling that investment now. Logic would tell you that if you are not willing to buy it now, why are you willing to hold it? In this scenario, chances are that you are holding on to it because you hope that it will go back to what you once had, and that is the wrong reason to own it.

For each time you answered yes, you would buy this investment again if you had cash, consider holding. If you would be willing to buy it again now, then you must like what you have. If you do not know what to do, consider selling half.

Once you have identified which investments you no longer want to own and have thought about whether you want to sell them, please note that before making any such moves, it is always wise to contact a tax advisor or another professional to be sure that the move makes sense for you in your current situation.

If one of the investments that you listed is a life insurance policy and if you have come to the conclusion that you want to replace this particular policy with another type of life insurance policy, please be sure that you have the new policy in place before you drop the old one. If you are simply dropping a policy because you are sure that you do not need insurance at all, do not do so until you have had a medical checkup to make sure that you are in perfect health.

ACT FROM YOUR CURRENT
STARTING POINT

Again, the law of looking at what you have applies to more than your money; it applies to every aspect of your life. It does not matter if you were once in love with the man or woman of your dreams; that man or woman is gone, and you must go on from here. It does not matter if you used to weigh 120; you now weigh 170 pounds and must decide what to do about it from here. It does not matter that you once were debt-free; you now have $15,000 worth of credit card debt, and you need to take action from here. (I'll say more about how to do this in Law 4.) It does not matter that a few years ago you had $200,000 in your retirement account; you now have $150,000, and you have to make decisions that will help that money grow from here. In relationships, in your work, in money, in weight, looking only at what you had instead of what you have will not let you create that which you really want. If you live in yesterday, you will never be able to get to where you want to be tomorrow. So if you always look at what you have, recognize and, most important, deal with it honestly, you will always open the way to tomorrow.

LESSONS FROM LAW 2:
LOOK AT WHAT YOU HAVE, NOT AT WHAT YOU HAD

+ There's nothing constructive about habitually comparing yourself and your money to something that no longer exists.

+ You are what you do today, not what you did yesterday.

+ No one rescues us—except ourselves.

+ You must have an accurate starting point for dealing with what is really going on and for taking the necessary actions to get you to where you want to be. That starting point must be today.

+ The past has no power over you unless you give it power.

+ Inability to accept the loss of anything you had is what keeps you from recognizing the gains that you have already made.

+ The fear of loss causes greater losses.

+ Denial of your present-day financial reality—your reality right now—is one of the biggest obstacles to wealth, both financial wealth and every other kind.

+ In hundreds of circumstances and dozens of ways, people hang on to the past to the detriment of their future.

+ The purpose of investing is to help your life go forward from where you are. You cannot go forward by looking back.

+ The easiest way to go forward is to look at where you are and at what you have and decide where you want to go from here.

+ The road to wealth isn't paved with what you once had. It's created out of what you do have and how you use it.

+ If you live in yesterday, you will never be able to get to where you want to be tomorrow.

DO WHAT IS RIGHT FOR YOU *BEFORE* YOU DO WHAT IS RIGHT FOR YOUR MONEY

*T*he principle at the heart of this law is tied in with the Second Commandment, which forbids us from putting graven images or idols (or love of money) before our consideration of a power of greater importance. In a similar way, you, your spirit, and your happiness are in my opinion far more important than your money. I'm sure you would agree with this. In fact, this law helps you realize that the true goal of money is not simply to make more with the money you have, but to help you feel financially secure, safe, protected, and happy. Your money should guard and take care of you; your primary job is not to guard and tend your money. And you *know* how fervently I believe that you *must* pay attention to your money and take care of it, in order for your money to be able to take care of you, so you see what an important law this is to understand.

Since you've learned to tell the truth about your money and now know to look only at what you have, you're ready to learn to do what's right for you *before* you do what's right for your money. Remember: You first, your spirit first, people first, *before* money.

Law 3 is also the most personal law in this book. Everyone has different tastes and styles—of dress and investing. You have your own emotional threshold for financial risk, reward, safety, uncertainty, and satisfaction. If you always count on others to tell you what is best for you to do in your life and with your money, you may very likely live a life in which *you* have been left out of the equation.

In the previous two laws, we saw that when it comes to the actions you take with your money, there are cut-and-dried guidelines: Is it true or false? Are you living in the past or the present? Here, however, the thought processes and the actions that result from following this law will be unique to *you*. For though this is a universal truth, the solution to your own particular money problems or questions will be highly individual.

Over the course of your lifetime, you will meet many different people and you will also *become* many different people. Most likely, you will find that your individual circumstances, income, desires, and goals will change. As they do, you will need to make financial decisions from new and different perspectives. If you are young and ambitious, for example, you may want to take on student loans to help you pursue your dreams—even though the idea of beginning your adult life with that much debt is daunting. If you take a partner in life and want that partnership to succeed and be harmonious, you will have to make many of your financial decisions according to what is best for both of you.

If you have children, they will become a priority in financial planning for twenty years or more. As you get older, your financial timetable will change too. You will still need to make choices out of a realistic understanding of today's circumstances, see the truth about your present, and keep an eye out for the future.

You will also need to plan for your or your partner's death.

Who are you, financially speaking? That is a difficult question, because the answer depends on your age, assets, goals, earnings, tax bracket, and financial obligations. Who are you "nonfinancially"? That question can be difficult to answer too, because it involves your character, dreams, and emotions. Yet this answer plays a crucial—perhaps the most crucial—role in the financial decisions that you make.

SUZE'S LESSON

LIFE IS PRECIOUS

The best way to let you see how strongly I believe in Law 3 is to share with you some of the profound experiences I have had with it. To me, these prove the truth of this universal principle.

One of my book tours ended on the night of September 10, 2001. I had been all over the country for two months, talking to thousands and thousands of people about the stock market, the economy, and what we could expect next. I had not been back to my apartment in New York City for at least seven weeks and was looking forward to it more than I can say. I was to leave on September 11 to fly back to the city from West Chester, Pennsylvania, via helicopter. I was excited about taking the helicopter ride because it provided one of the most beautiful scenes in the world as it flew past the World Trade Center, over all the other buildings, and landed on Thirty-fourth Street, right next to the East River. God, what a sight that was.

Yet that morning as I was packing to leave, the first plane hit the World Trade Center and the world stopped in its tracks.

The next day, I managed to drive back to New York, seeing in the distance the terrible cloud of smoke towering over the city. I had been called by friends at CNBC to appear on some of their shows to talk about what we could expect to happen to our money and what we should do. When I arrived in the studio's green room, one of my fellow guests asked, "Suze, what are we going to tell everyone?" I looked at him and said, "Just tell them the truth. But more important, love them with your words." The truth was that none of us, regardless of our financial or political expertise and accomplishments, could know the effects that this incomprehensible event would really have on our economy or our fellow citizens' money.

So we went on the air to talk, but we didn't really talk about money. The market hadn't opened up yet; money wasn't moving; people we loved were lost. All we could talk about was what to do about our lives, to talk about what is important in life, to tell the truth. I picked every single word I used with such thought and care because I believed that if we just supported one another in every way possible, we would get through that crisis.

The following March, I got a call from my lecture agent, Carol, who had been contacted by a woman named Vinnie who had lost her husband, Joey, a fireman, in the terrorist attack. Vinnie had asked if I would be willing to come speak to the widows, widowers, and loved ones of the firemen who had been killed. Of course I would—I wanted to do anything I could to help. The date was set and one morning I went to a hotel in New York to meet with a number of the wives, husbands, dads, children, and friends of the deceased firefighters.

That was the hardest talk of my life. How do you look into the eyes of an entire audience filled with really good people who had just lost their husbands, mothers, fathers, daughters or sons and talk to them about what to do with the money that they would receive or had received as a result of a terrible tragedy? Most of the people in the room hated the money they had gotten. They did not want it. They wanted their sons and daughters back. They wanted their husbands and wives back. They wanted their fathers and mothers back. They would have traded all the "blood money," as one woman called it, just to have their loved ones with them again. One young mother stood in the back of the room through the whole four-hour talk holding a three-month-old baby, whose Papa had obviously never gotten to see him and who would never get to see his papa. She stood there rocking back and forth, holding that child as if he were her past, her present, and her future—all that mattered to her.

During those four hours, those who had come to seek help revealed that they had started doing things with their money that they had never done before. For many (especially the wives in the room), their husbands' pensions and the money from the relief funds put them in a situation where they were getting more monthly income than they had received when their husbands were alive. Most of these families had just barely been making it before 9/11 and they now were millionaires. Some had gotten $500,000 or $1 million or more in a lump sum. Not only were they having to deal with the loss of their loved ones, they were also dealing with the fact that they now had the largest amount of money that they had ever had in their lives— all because they had lost the person they loved most.

One woman had just gone out and bought $15,000 worth of clothes, something she had never ever done before. She didn't need them and didn't know why she'd bought them. Another was going to buy a house on the ocean, but when I asked her why, she said, "Because *his* dream was always to have a house on the water." Another wanted help with a friend who was still too shattered to come to hear me that day but who was walking around with $900,000 worth of checks crumpled up in her purse as if they were worthless pieces of paper. A daughter was there so that she could learn to help her mom, who was still having trouble leaving the house except to go to Kmart, because that is where she and her husband used to shop all the time. When I asked what her mother went to find at Kmart, she answered, "My dad."

Story after story, tear after tear, my bottom-line advice to each and every person in that room was: "You have to learn to do what is right for *you* first. Then and only then we will learn what is right for you to do with your money."

After we talked more about their feelings, what it was like for all of them to have to wake up every day and carry on with their lives, what it meant to them to do what was right for them in this situation, then we were finally ready to address what they should do (for now, anyway) with their newfound wealth.

I knew that the majority of people in that room would not be able to comprehend very much just then about the actions I was telling them to take with their money, because they were still in such a state of deep shock and grief. So the financial advice that I gave them was very direct and very simple: "I want you to take this money and pay off all your debts. If you have the money to do so, that includes your mortgage, credit card debt, car loans, and student loans. The bottom line is, *all of your debt has got to go.* After you have done that, I want you to put the money you have left in a money market fund until you feel your heart is ready to start making other money moves." I knew this task would be easy for all of them to do, financially speaking, because we had discussed their debt load and how much money they had recently received. When I asked if anyone in the room felt it would be a financial strain to do this, no one raised a hand.

I then went on and warned them that, in my experience with dealing with clients who had lost a loved one, the healing of the heart takes a good year or more to happen, so they needed to be patient with themselves in the process. They were not to worry about letting their money sit in a place that was safe and sound, such as a money market fund or a federally insured savings account. I also wanted to make sure that, when they were ready to invest, they would not be tempted to make any of the very common mistakes that people make with their money. So I gave them a list of investments they should always avoid. They had already suffered enough loss; I didn't want them to suffer a financial loss, too. So I gave them my "Investment Hate List" and made them write it down and repeat it to me out loud:

+ No variable annuities, especially in a retirement account
+ No whole life insurance policies
+ No universal life insurance policies
+ No variable life insurance policies
+ No mutual funds that carry a load (A shares or B shares)
+ No bond funds (especially intermediate or long-term bond funds)

This list is important for you, too. So please take note of these recommendations in your guidebook when you review your own investments.

We talked about how if they did not currently have a revocable living trust and a will in place they needed to get one as soon as possible. They needed this now more than ever, because many of them had become single parents and had to take steps to make sure they were protecting their kids and, then, of course, their money. Without a will and trust, on their own death the lawyers might get a good chunk of their money. I had to ask them hard questions, such as, "Who would take care of your kids if something happened to you? Who would take care of your kids' money? Here you are at the age of twenty, thirty, forty and you don't have a clue about what to do with the money you just got. What do you think your kids would do with it?" I explained that if they did not have the right documents in place, not only were they jeopardizing their kids' financial future, but a good portion of this money might also be lost, unnecessarily. So, again, they had to do what was right for them, for their kids, and *then* for their money.

In the aftermath of 9/11, my focus—and the focus of many other financial advisors—has been on "people first, then money." It should not have taken two buildings coming down in the middle of New York City to get us back in touch with this natural law.

Please understand, as much as I love to teach about money and talk about the laws of money, none of that would even matter if you were not here. So let's take care of you first, then take care of those you love. We must never forget that a human life is the most important thing in this world. Without you in your world, nothing else would exist.

WHAT DOES IT MEAN TO DO WHAT IS RIGHT FOR YOU *BEFORE* YOU DO WHAT IS RIGHT FOR YOUR MONEY?

Over the years, I have continually examined what Law 3 really means and tried to answer questions about how you know what is right for you, especially when you are talking about money. Is buying a stock only right if you buy a stock and it goes up? How do you know if it is right for you to go into a money market fund *instead of* a good, diversified stock portfolio? Is it right to keep the house that you love, even if you do not have the money to pay for it or any of your other bills? Is it right for you to follow your dreams, even if that means living on much less than you ever expected? Maybe yes, maybe no.

In a nutshell, what I have learned is that this law means that before you look at financial decisions—at stocks, homes, cars, college education—you have to know *and do* what feels right to you, what feels safe for you, what empowers you, what helps you grow, and what works for you emotionally and mentally. After all that, then you really *do* have the ability to make intelligent moves with your money.

If you know what you feel about yourself and your money in this moment, then you tend not to buy or sell stocks at the wrong time, you are not tempted to purchase something that would get you further into debt, and you rarely make financial decisions that would jeopardize your financial future. When you know what is right for you, the answers to your money questions— stocks, mutual funds, new purchases—are all obvious and correct *for you*. Sure, you may get scared and uncertain and be tempted to sell quickly. Or you may feel desperate because of losses and thus be tempted by a tip that promises a sure thing. But if you follow the guidelines above and in the rest of this chapter and go through the guidebook at the end of the book, you will be better able to quell those emotions so that you do what's right for you.

YOUR FINANCIAL FINGERPRINTS

Each person has a set of financial priorities that are right just for him. Just as no one has your fingerprints, so no one has your particular way of living life, handling money, or making decisions. Everyone is different.

When we stop comparing ourselves to others, we can really accept who we are and who others are much more easily. And once we accept who we are, we can make decisions about our money based on our makeup—our need for safety, our tolerance for fear and risk, the amount of worry we generate, our optimism, and our pessimism. It's all part of the "you" that we are talking about in "do what is right for *you*." Doing what is right is easy once you know *who* you are. But if you don't know who you are, nothing you do with your money will ever feel right.

CHRIS'S LESSON

YOUR MONEY MUST CREATE PEACE OF MIND FOR YOU, NOT EXTRA ANXIETY

Imagine that you are sitting by yourself in a restaurant. In the next booth, two women are in such a heated conversation about money that you cannot help overhearing every word they say.

CHRIS: I just can't stand it anymore. Every time I open my retirement account statement and look at my investments, I want to run screaming out the door. There isn't a single stock that has gone up from where I purchased it, and over the last four years I have lost more than $100,000 of what I had. I couldn't afford to lose this money. What if something had happened to the business? What am I going to do? Even though the market is going up, my investments haven't gone up at all. I don't even want to look at the statements anymore. They come, and I feel like using them as packing material in the boxes I'm going to need when I have to move out of my home, which I will not be able to afford anymore when I retire because of all the money I have lost. I talk to the financial advisor who put me in these investments, but that does not help one bit. He's a great guy, and he thought that he was doing right by me, I suppose, but now I can barely stand to talk to him either. All he says is, "Listen, I like the stocks you're in, but if you don't and want to sell them, let's sell." But then I get afraid, because what if they go back up? So I don't know what to do. I'm driving myself crazy, Amy. It was not supposed to be like this. I just don't get how come you're not freaking out about your money.

AMY: I don't know, Chris, but I'm not. Listen, just like yourself, my investments are down too, but for some reason, and I'm not even sure why, it doesn't bother me. I look at my statements and somehow I just figure that, in time, they will be okay. I think they're good investments. The companies have been around forever, but the truth is, Who knows anymore for sure today? I have decided just to trust it. It somehow feels all right to me. Hey, don't get me wrong. It's not like I love losing money and I don't wish the markets would go up—I do. But overall, hey, I'm okay. Maybe it's because when I talk to Jules at the brokerage firm, I believe him when he reminds me why I made the investments in the first place. So, Chris, I have decided just to stay the

course. As for the business—well, I'm going to give
it all I have and make sure it is a success so that I
don't have to pack and move out when I retire, and
I suggest that you do the same thing.

———

ONE SIZE DOES NOT FIT ALL

What do you imagine are the differences between Chris and
Amy when it comes to how they've invested their money?
    Circle yes or no for the following questions:

Do you think that Amy owns better stocks
and mutual funds than Chris does?   Yes/No
Do you think that Amy is doing better in
her business than Chris is?   Yes/No
Do you think that if Chris were invested
in the same stocks and funds that Amy
owns she would feel differently about
her investments?   Yes/No
Do you think that if Chris used the same
advisor and brokerage firm that Amy
uses she would feel better?   Yes/No

What answers did you circle? I would bet that you circled yes
to every one of those questions. Most people, including many
financial advisors, would assume that if Chris is unhappy, she
must have made bad investments, had a bad broker or a bad
firm, or all of the above. However, if you are going to write a fiscal prescription, maybe you had better get to know the patient—
yourself—a little better.

In this case, here are some important facts about Chris and Amy:

+ Chris and Amy are business partners, fifty-fifty, so if one's business goes down, so does the other's.
+ The money they are talking about is money they have each put into their firm's retirement account.
+ They both started with exactly the same amount of money.
+ They both use Jules, the same investment advisor.
+ They both bought exactly the same stocks in exactly the same amounts at exactly the same time.
+ The balances in their accounts are currently identical.
+ The income they take home from the business they share is identical.

Why, then, does Amy feel all right about what has happened to her money and Chris does not? Simply put, Chris is *not* Amy. Chris is Chris, with all that goes with that—her fears, her confidence, her optimism. The only real solution for Chris will be to find out what *she* thinks is right for *her* first, then her money, and work with that. Let's see how to write the perfect fiscal prescription for Chris using Law 3.

The Fiscal Cure

Amy, who had done some work with me on her finances, asked if I would talk to Chris and try to help her. I said of course. It was the week before Thanksgiving 2002 by the time all three of us were able to connect. Amy and I both were expecting that Chris would be feeling better about her finances, since almost three months had passed since their heated exchange. By that time, the markets had had a really great run and had gone almost straight up for seven weeks—and most likely were going to have a great run in 2003.

But that did not matter to Chris. She still was an emotional wreck over her money. She had told us that she had gained a serious amount of weight, her health was deteriorating, she hadn't been watching where she was going and had stumbled into a pothole and sprained her ankle and wrenched her back. She was sore but okay, even though her life seemed to be falling apart.

As we talked to Chris, we went through all her money—investments, savings, insurance, expenses—from top to bottom. We then went through Chris's emotions from top to bottom, and bottom to top. What made her afraid? What would make her feel secure? What were her personal goals? Did she care more about how she felt or how much money she had? This was not easy for Chris to articulate, because no one had ever asked her these sorts of questions about her money. And of course I did not let her evade any of the questions when she did not know the answer. I made her stick with it until she could answer it before we would go on.

After all was said and done, Chris herself decided that to stop feeling afraid and begin to take the right actions for herself first and then with her money—she had to sell about 75 percent of the investments in her retirement accounts right now. She came to that amount by using the Fear Factor Scale (see page 79). By selling 75 percent of what she had that day, she knew she would be okay, financially speaking, no matter what happened with the 25 percent that remained invested in the stock market. She realized that even if she just invested that 75 percent in bonds yielding 5 percent, as long as nothing happened to those bonds, she would be just fine.

As soon as she made that decision, we made a conference call to Amy's and Chris's broker, Jules, and told him of her decisions. Jules did not try to talk her out of it, but agreed with her all the way. And I knew that could not be easy for him—he had two people on the phone who owned exactly the same stocks, one who wanted to sell and one who wanted to stay invested. So you see how this law plays out? While Chris's decision was the right one for her and she was selling, Amy was thinking about buying some more stock. Same stocks, different people, different moves, different results. We all listened as Chris and Jules decided together which stocks would be the best for Chris to sell, which she should keep, and which safe bonds she should buy and why.

Notice that Chris did not just sell her stocks blindly. So, when you start to put this law into effect in your own life, I want you to undertake the same thoughtful, careful process that Chris did. First, she had to look really hard at what was right for her, given who she is and what she was feeling and needing in that moment. She took care of herself emotionally by using the financial Fear Factor Scale to decide how much she needed to safeguard so that she would not freak out anymore. Only then did she shift her attention to how best to carry out her decision, and she was able to do what was right for her money by getting some solid advice from Jules.

WHEN IT COMES TO MONEY, PARENTS FIRST—THEN KIDS

When you do start to learn what is right for you, especially if you are a mother or father, sometimes the "you" goes out the window. For you know and I know that parents will do anything for their child even when it is *not* the best thing for themselves. We have to look at this together, because *even* as a parent, you have to take care of yourself first. It's been said so often that it's a cliché, but it's still useful, so I'm going to say it here just as the airlines say it before every flight: "In the event of an emergency, oxygen masks will drop from the compartment above you. Put your own mask on first, then put the mask on your child." You have to take care of yourself if you're going to be any help to your child.

One of the questions I am asked most frequently is something like this one, which one woman asked me at a lecture not long ago: "Suze, I'm a single mother and I feel so guilty because I haven't started saving for my eight-year-old daughter's college education. How do I do that?" Here's what I asked her in return:

Are you free of credit card debt? *No.*

Do you have any money saved for your retirement? *No.*

Do you have an emergency fund in case you cannot work? *No.*

Do you have the right insurance in place in case something happens to you? *No.*

This woman feels guilty and ashamed that she has not started to save for her child's education, but she says nothing about the fears that she has about her own life.

MAKING THE WRONG CHOICE

With the high cost of education today, not just college but also private and parochial high schools and grammar schools, it really is almost impossible for many parents to shoulder educational expenses—unless their children can get scholarships or are willing to take out student loans. I know that you do not want your kids to have to start out life saddled with debt. But I want you to listen to me about this: You cannot mortgage your home or take money from your retirement accounts just to make sure that your kids do not have to start out their adult life in debt in order to finish college. You must not do anything and everything you can to send them to college if it means destroying your own financial health. This is a big, big mistake and in direct violation of Law 3.

MAYA'S LESSON

Ignorance Is Not Bliss, Nor Is It Financially Good in the Long Run

Let me tell you a story about what can happen if you don't obey the law of taking care of yourself first. Listen to Maya's story:

> I was so excited when my mom told me of course I could go to Juilliard and I wouldn't have to worry about money. She said, "I've always told you we would pay for it and we will." I couldn't wait to call all my friends and tell them that I was going to the school of my dreams. Juilliard is an incredibly exclusive school in New York City where you have to be a really good musician or performer to get in. The competition for spots is fierce. I was never sure whether my parents could really afford a school like that or not. I was fine with taking out student loans, because I knew that was how a lot of kids had to pay for college, but when I'd bring it up with my mom, she would ask, "Will your other friends have to take out student loans?" And when I'd say no, she'd say, "Well, then, neither will you. Case closed."
>
> I always sensed that we didn't have as much money as the kids I went to high school with, but no one in the family would ever talk about it—about money. Even though Mom had always said that they would pay for college, Juilliard was a private school to the tune of

about $25,000 a year, plus the major expense of living in New York. So, when they said no problem, I just assumed that they must know what they're doing. But still I just could not believe it when the acceptance letter did come and Mom still said I could go.

I rented an apartment in Manhattan with some friends and went with them to buy furniture and supplies as well as all the cool clothes that I wanted to be seen in. I charged all that on my mom's credit card. I guess I should have noticed that something was not quite right because every time my mom gave me a credit card to use it was a brand-new one.

When the time came and I trotted off to my first year of college, I thought everything was so great. The years flew by for me and I just loved everything about New York and the school. We were approaching graduation and, as I was talking to my mom about what were we going to do to celebrate, she did not really want to talk about it. Every time we did talk she got more and more tense, as if I had done something wrong. She also cried a lot but never would tell me why. When my dad would come into New York to visit me, he would tell me not to worry about mom, that she was just going through a phase.

It wasn't until my parents came to my graduation that I finally got that something was really wrong. We had the greatest day and I was so proud to go up there and get my degree. That night we went out to dinner with about fifteen of my friends and their parents and my mom and dad picked up the bill. The next day we were sitting on the grass in Central Park, and Mom asked me if I was still going to come back to New Jersey and work for the summer like I always did. I told her that in fact I had decided a few days before to stay in New York with my boyfriend and just hang out with him and take a break. Well, with those words I thought World War Three had started. "What do you mean you're just going to hang out? Do you think your father and I got ourselves into this kind of debt just so you can hang with your boyfriend and take a break?" I said, "Mom, what are you talking about?" She was still so angry that she couldn't hear a word I was saying. She kept going on and on about what an ungrateful child I was, then burst into tears. My dad and I just stared at her as she huffed off and said she would meet us back at my apartment.

On that walk back, my dad and I didn't say one word. They left to drive home about an hour later. What a way to end four great years at college.

After they left, I called one of my friends back home to tell her what happened and she said, "Oh, is that why there is a For Sale sign on your home?" I said "What?!" She said, "Yeah, the sign has been up for about three weeks now." I hung up and called my mom but my parents hadn't gotten home yet, so I left a message to call me. The next day she called to say she was so sorry and hadn't meant to ruin my day. But I said, "Please, level with me. What's up? Why are you selling the house?" She asked who'd told me and when I didn't answer, said, "Listen, here's the story." Then it all just poured out of her.

MAYA'S MOM

Years ago we were doing very well, your father was making a lot of money, we had saved a nice sum, and then everything seemed to go wrong. When we moved to the new neighborhood, we thought we would eventually start to make more money so that we could afford this house as well as the vacation home we still had. But that didn't happen.

Your father's business started to get in trouble, so, to keep it going, we used up our savings. You were the most important thing in the world to us and we wanted to give you the best. So we did, always thinking that things would turn around for us. We just kept spending money like everything was okay, but it never did turn around. Remember how we tried to sell the vacation home? And how I started teaching those art classes? That is because we had no sources of money left. I had been robbing Peter to pay Paul and here we are ten years later and there is no one left to rob.

Your father and I are in serious financial trouble. We're over $70,000 in credit card debt. We've borrowed everything we already could over all these years from Dad's parents. We're three months behind in our mortgage payments. Our car just broke down and we have no money to fix it. We've maxed out on our credit cards and we can't even afford to pay the minimum on most of them. The vacation home has still not sold and we've already taken out all the equity from it as well as from the house we live in and can't make the payments on them either. We just got hit with a tax bill saying we owed back taxes; with penalties, that bill comes to over $100,000. Your father has been out of work for almost five years, and finally he's had to take a job paying eight dollars an hour at a collection agency. We have $17,000 a month in bills because of all the creditors we owe money to. And all we have coming in is about $2,500 a month between the two of us. We're about to lose this house, our vacation house, and we have nothing at all to fall back on. So here we are at the age of fifty, in such hot water that our only option is to put this house up for sale to give us some money to live on. We found a small, one-bedroom apartment we can take when our house sells and we'll just try to take it one day at a time.

After Maya heard this grim history of her parents' finances, she felt horrible at the thought of all the money they had spent on her—at least $200,000 on the schooling for college, and a large fraction of that for her private high school. On top of that, she had taken trips with friends, bought clothes she hadn't really needed, and spent so much—putting all of these expenses on her parents' credit cards. She felt that she was a major cause of her parents' losing everything. She would have gladly gone out and gotten student loans, and perhaps would have thought twice about going to Juilliard to get her degree if she had known the real state of her family's finances. She felt betrayed that they hadn't had the faith in her to tell her the truth about their financial situation. But mainly she just felt stupid that she had not seen all the financial warning signs, which looked so obvious as she thought back on them.

Not So Unusual

I am sure as you read Maya's lesson, you were wondering whether all that could happen to just one couple. In fact, while the names and sometimes the locations are different, all the stories in this book, including Maya's, are true. This book reveals the lessons we learn in life that money somehow seems always

to teach us. Maya's situation is not that unusual. Her parents—
and many other mothers and fathers around the world—are living in direct violation of all the laws of money, especially Law 3.

———

HOW TO TAKE CARE OF YOURSELF AND YOUR CHILDREN

As you may have started to notice, when you are in violation of
one law you usually are in violation of all of them. Let's look at
these first three laws, for example:

*   Maya's parents were not telling Maya or the world the truth
    about who they really were (Law 1).
*   Maya's parents were spending money as if they still had it and
    not in accordance with what they currently have (Law 2).
*   Maya's parents were not doing what was right for them on
    any level and their money was showing it (Law 3).

How could it have been different if Maya's parents had been
abiding by the laws of money? They would have chosen from
the start to tell Maya the truth. They would also have prepared
Maya for the fact that she would most likely have to go to a
community college or a state school; get student loans on her
own; or get really great grades so that she could get a scholar-
ship—otherwise, college would not be possible. Finally, they
would have told Maya that she was going to have to work during high school, because they needed her to pay for some of her
expenses.

Do you think that if her parents had shared any of these
truths with her, Maya would have failed in life? No, she would
not have. She would have made it just fine. Maybe she would

have gone on to be even greater than she will be now, for now she is weighed down with the guilt and the incredible confusion caused by the years of pent-up anger from her parents—especially her mom—over a situation that her parents chose to put themselves in.

YOUR TRUE FINANCIAL ACHILLES' HEEL

Do you know what Maya's parents' true Achilles' heel was when it came to their money? It was that they did not know how to do both: take care of themselves *and* fulfill their desire to help their child. So they took themselves out of the equation. And Maya's parents might be no different from you.

The fact that so many parents are not putting their own financial health first is a huge problem in America today. For this reason, it is very important that we look a little more closely at the reasons that Maya's parents may have chosen to put themselves in financial jeopardy. Their actions were not those of mean or selfish people. Theirs were the actions of parents who love their child more than they love themselves and who were under the widely shared illusion that parents must take care of their children's entire future, rather than find a way for the whole family to work on their future together.

DOUBLE JEOPARDY

Even though I know that this concept may be difficult for you to accept, I very much want you to see that you do not need to jeopardize your own financial future in order to guard your child's health and well-being. Can you also see that sometimes when you think you are sacrificing your own well-being to help someone else, in the long run you may be in fact hurting him or her? For instance, Maya is terribly hurt because her parents didn't take her into their trust nor allow her to help them with what they had and what they did not have.

So if you are in a situation where it is a severe strain on your finances to be able to pay for your children's education, here are a few questions to consider:

- Have you told the truth to your children about your financial situation from the beginning?
- Have you prepared your children to share the responsibility for the cost of their education?
- Do they understand that they must do their part—perhaps to get good grades and to think about community colleges and state schools—while you do your part, making sure that you all can eat, stay safe and warm, and have a roof over your heads?
- Have you let them know how much you love them and that, together, you will find a way for them to achieve the most in their lives, even if it is not the way their friends are doing it?

If the answer to any of these questions is no, it's time to bring your children into the conversation and for *you* to start doing what is right for you. They are never too young to learn how to take some responsibility for themselves and their future, nor too old to know that you will be there for them as parents and partners. And it is never too late for you, either, to take responsibility for yourself and your future.

I am not saying that you should not help your children to get an education. My point is that you cannot do it at your expense— and by your expense I mean that you cannot destroy your own financial life to pay for that which you can't afford.

Have I made my point? You *must* learn to live by this law. To do what is right for you means that you include yourself and your children in the same equation, and that you never make yourselves financially vulnerable. It means explaining to your children early on what it takes to get an education. And if your children are about to enter school, it means that you must talk to them honestly as soon as possible about how you and they *together* can make it work—without significant hardship.

FINANCES, NOT FANTASY

One of the hardest things about Law 3 is best explained by looking at the situation that Maya has found herself in. What can she do now to take care of herself first? She has taken on the guilt and blame for her parents' debt, even though it's not her fault. Maya didn't force her parents to destroy themselves financially, but she wants to try to pay them back for her education.

Maya also worries about how she's going to get a job as a musician and support herself. While it is true that she will have to earn money somehow, it doesn't mean that she has to give up what is right for her in the long run. Maya has to hold on to her own dreams. (You have to do the same, but you do this not by holding them as a fantasy, but by taking practical steps to make them a reality.)

What is right for Maya now? The most important thing for her is to take care of her finances, so she can make her dreams come true someday. That means she needs to make sure she's covering the basics, that she has enough money to live. In short, she needs income, pronto. So Maya needs to get a job, even if it is not the dream career that she just prepared for. Any job will do at first. Even if she starts an office job, she can perform at night in clubs while looking out for that one opening that will allow her to live her dream as a musician.

Doing what is right for you includes being realistic about your situation. Doing what is right for you means knowing what your real financial needs are and how you are going to meet them. Doing what is right for you means never just living off of fantasy instead of finance. Doing what is right for you means keeping your dreams alive until one day you find yourself living them.

To do what is right for you, you need to get out of credit card debt.

IS CREDIT CARD DEBT GOOD FOR YOU?

An enormous number of people have credit card debt. If you are one of them, I want you to know that you are not alone. Almost everyone I talk to is in that situation. Law 3 applies to you if you are young and just starting out, if you have a huge student loan to pay off, or if you are so deep in debt that you cannot even pay what's required to keep the credit cards and there is absolutely no end in sight, and you are also worried about paying the electric bill.

Before I tell you how it applies to you, I want you to look at an example.

THE BALANCING ACT

You walk into a store, and there is a great coat on sale and you cannot afford it, but you love it and it's totally right for you. So you charge it on your credit card and believe that somehow the money thing will work out. You say, "Oh, Suze says I must do what is right for me. Suze said it's a law!" And then you think,

"This coat would really make me happy, lift my spirits, and keep me warm." So you buy it.

Listen, it's true that this law says, "Do what is right for you," but it also says, "Do what is right for your money." So even though that bit with the coat was a nice try, when you think like this, both your thought processes and your action violate the law. What is right for you will, in the long run, also always be right for your money. In this case, the coat is wrong for your money, because you cannot afford it. And it is also wrong for you, because doing the right thing for yourself will *never* mean putting the things you buy before money, and it will *never* put you in unnecessary consumer debt, leaving you to pay for a coat long after you stop wearing it. The point of this law is that you have to have ownership over your finances. You have to become attuned to your money.

In fact, the reason you got into debt in the first place was by violating this law. If you knew inside what was really right for you, you wouldn't spend money you didn't have. *If you are in debt, the only thing that is right for you is to get out of debt . . . now.* Credit card debt is bondage, and you will never be able to keep what you have or create what you deserve if you are in bondage. There is no way it can be right for you to be in bondage. . . . How could it be right for you to walk yourself into a living prison with no date of release?

The truth is, if you apply this law and ask yourself, "Is another purchase right for me at this moment?" and if you really are honest with yourself and look at what you have, you *know* you don't want any more debt. You want to be free. So yes, this law applies to you and to anyone in any financial situation. I go into great detail about the financial actions you can take to get out of debt in the next chapter, on Law 4, and within the guidebook in the back.

CREATING BALANCE FOR YOURSELF

In some ways, we can think of Law 3 as balancing your own financial scale. On the one side, you weigh the intangibles, like peace of mind, fear, security, and comfort. On the other, you weigh the tangibles: new investments, new house, more debt. And you try to create a balance for yourself.

But balancing your individual financial scale—by doing what is right for yourself as well as what is right for your money—is not easy to achieve. You need to be very honest with yourself. And as I said at the beginning of this chapter, there is no one universal right answer and this law is extremely personal. The decisions you make each time will be uniquely your own.

PUTTING THE LAW TO WORK

So now that we have seen some examples of other people's financial lives, the question is: How do *you* know whether or not you feel okay about a financial action you might take in your own life? Knowing what is right for you means choosing that which will create harmony in your life. It is choosing what will protect you in the long run. You'll know you've found what's right for you because you'll *feel* it. You'll feel in sync with your life and in sync with your money.

One way to help you discover your level of comfort and harmony with a financial action and decision is to use the Fear Factor Scale at the end of this chapter. But before you do that, you need to make a real assessment of your own principles, of who you are and how you view your money.

MY GOAL FOR YOUR MONEY

It is very important that you understand that my goal for your money is not just to make you more money, which I mentioned at the outset of this chapter. For instance, even though when I called Chris about her money worries the market had been going up for seven straight weeks and she was starting to make more money (on paper, anyway), if she had hung on to those stocks, she would have continued to lose her quality of life because of the anxiety she felt. It's not that she was right and Amy was wrong. Finding what is right for you is not about making someone else out to be wrong. It's a highly personal process.

I think the goal of money is to make you feel more secure, to give you more freedom, and to let you have more control over your life. And that is exactly what started to happen to Chris as soon as she sold. So what you need to know is, what makes you secure? What makes you insecure?

YOUR EXERCISE

Chris had to answer some hard questions about herself and her relationship to her money so that she could get in touch with the actions she needed to take *for* herself *before* she took action with her money. So do you. Therefore, here or in the guidebook, start to ask yourself the following questions:

- What makes you feel secure when it comes to your money?
- What makes you happy when you think about your finances?
- What makes you afraid about your future and your money?
- What is your greatest financial fear?

You are fooling yourself if you think that money is more powerful than your emotions. It is important that you find out the answers to these questions, so please make sure you answer them truthfully, clearly, and fully. Answer each one in full before you move to the next one, as I made Chris do.

Obviously, a lot more goes into investing your money than this and we will address that in the next chapter. But this is the first action that you must take to stay in accordance with Law 3. You need to know the basic principles by which you live your life, principles that are unique to you. Otherwise, you will be out of sync with Law 3 and you will not be doing what is right for you *or* your money.

WE END WHERE WE STARTED

We started this chapter with a look back at some of the personal losses that came from the tragedy of 9/11. And at that time, and in the months after, on TV program after program, in emails and on the radio, I talked about how important it was to do what is right for ourselves and our loved ones.

Are you one of those people who promised, after the attacks, that you would take care of yourself; you would get those check-ups; you would take care of those you love; spend more time with your kids; make sure you have the correct amounts of term life insurance; take action to get or amend your will and your revocable trust; and put all your documents in order? You told me that you would put this law into effect in your life, that you would comply with it completely.

But here is what to this day is breaking my heart. Here we all are years after 9/11, and *have* you done what you said you were going to do? I suspect you have not. What is stopping you? The answer to that question is: You are. I am asking you again, please, do not ignore the life lessons that you have learned from this law. I am asking you to do what is right for you and for your loved ones; and I am asking you at least to try your best to do it *today*.

The Lessons from Law 3: Do What Is Right for You *Before* You Do What Is Right for Your Money

✢ It is necessary to put yourself first when it comes to making your financial decisions.

✢ The goal for your money is not just to make more money. The goal of money is to make you feel more secure, to give you more freedom, and to let you take more control over your life.

✢ The main point of this law is that money is a mirror. When you do what's right for you, it shows up in your money. When you don't do what's right for you, it also shows up in your money.

✢ Over the course of your lifetime, you will meet many different people and you will also *become* many different people.

✢ You must never forget: a human life is the most important thing in this world. Without you in your world, nothing else would exist.

✢ Each person has his or her own set of financial priorities that are right just for him or her. Just as no one has your fingerprints, no one has your particular way of living life, handling money, or making decisions. Everyone is different.

✢ When you stop comparing yourself to others, you can really accept who you are and who others are much more easily.

And once you accept who you are, you can make decisions about your money based on your makeup–your need for safety, your tolerance for fear and risk, the amount of worry you generate, your optimism, and your pessimism.

✦ Doing what is right is easy once you know *who* you are. But if you don't know who you are, nothing you do with your money will ever feel right.

LESSONS FOR PARENTS

✦ You cannot mortgage your home or take money from your retirement accounts, just to make sure that your kids do not have to finish college and start adult life in debt. You must not do anything and everything you can to send them to college if it means destroying your own financial health.

✦ Children are never too young to learn how to take some responsibility for themselves and their future, and never too old to know that you will be there for them as parents and partners.

✦ To do what is right for you means that you include yourself and your children in the equation. Never do anything that makes you or your children financially vulnerable.

PUTTING LAW 3 INTO ACTION:
USING THE FEAR FACTOR SCALE

In the introduction, I said I would teach you how to rein in your fear about money. Fear, when it hits, can career out of control. It can paralyze you from taking action, especially the correct action. The way to rein in fear is to face it directly and take rational action. You don't want to ignore it; you don't want to act it out wildly. This Fear Factor Scale is one tool for reining in fear when working with your money.

From now on, when you are debating whether to take any important action with your money, such as investing in the stock market or selling investments you have, and you are confused about what to do, I want you to use this scale. Here's how it works.

CURRENT INVESTMENTS

1. Take out a piece of paper and write down numbers 1 through 5, horizontally, like this (or use the chart on pages 240–242 of the guidebook):

1 2 3 4 5

   These numbers make up your fear scale.
2. Write down in a column the name of every single investment that you currently have. Remember this scale is not just for real estate investments, stocks, mutual funds, or bonds, but also can be used for insurance products and any major purchase.
3. Ask yourself the following question about each investment and asset.

4. On a scale of 1 to 5, with 1 being no fear and 5 being fear to the point of losing sleep, how do you feel about each investment you currently own? Write the number down next to the investment in question.

5. If you are unsure which number to pick, use this list as a guide:

KEY TO FEAR FACTOR SCALE

CIRCLE THIS NUMBER ON YOUR LIST	IF YOU FEEL THIS WAY ABOUT OWNING THE INVESTMENT:
1	Absolutely fine; no problem whatsoever.
2	Fine, but a little bit unsure.
3	Not sure how you feel at all and it is causing you confusion about what to do.
4	Most of the time you feel sick about this investment, although once in a while you are okay with it.
5	This investment scares you to death; you can't stand to open the envelope that contains information about it, you wake up in the middle of the night thinking about it, or you are distracted by it when watching a movie.

6. Do this with every single one of your investments.

Now take a look at your list. If you are trying to decide if you should sell an investment and you have circled a number, this is what your Fear Factor Scale is indicating that you should do:

IF YOU CIRCLED	THE ACTION YOU TAKE FOR THIS INVESTMENT IS:
1	Keep it all.
2	Sell 25 percent.
3	Sell 50 percent.
4	Sell 75 percent.
5	Sell it all.

MAKING A NEW INVESTMENT

Do the same thing with any new investment or purchase you are considering making.

If you are using this scale to determine whether you should make an investment, remember: you can also ease into an investment over time. One big mistake we tend to make with our money is that we become all-or-nothing investors. (We'll talk more about that in Law 4.) We tend to either buy everything at once or sell everything at once. *You do not have to do everything at once.*

If you use the Fear Factor Scale to purchase an investment, this is how it will work:

1. Decide on the investment and the amount of money that you are thinking about investing in it. Let's say, for example, that your financial advisor has called you and told you about a great mutual fund. (Please use any amount in the following example.) Let's say that $10,000 of your money has been safe and sound in a money market fund, but since interest rates are so low on money market funds, he is suggesting that you take

that money and invest all $10,000 in the stock market via a mutual fund he recommends. It sounds good but you are not exactly sure this is what you want to do with all your money. Even though you have hesitations, you tell yourself that he must know what is good for your money. Right? Maybe he does, but maybe he doesn't. As Law 3 says, all that matters is whether it is right for you. How will it make you feel? If you invest and are scared to death and start losing sleep, then you are putting money *before* you and you are breaking this law.

2. If you are confused about what to do when making such an investment, please ask yourself the following question: If you were to take all $10,000 and put it in this investment right here and now how would it make you feel? Use the following table:

CIRCLE THIS NUMBER	IF YOU FEEL THIS WAY ABOUT MAKING THIS INVESTMENT:
1	You feel great and happy to buy it.
2	You have a very slight hesitation but mainly feel great about it.
3	You are really confused—you want to buy this, but at the same time you do not want to.
4	You have a slight desire to do it, but overall you really feel reluctant.
5	The thought of making this investment scares you to death, but you are afraid to miss out on what may be a great investment opportunity.

This is what the Fear Factor Scale is telling you with regard to your feeling about this investment:

IF YOU CIRCLED	THE ACTION YOU TAKE REGARDING THIS INVESTMENT IS:
1	You feel safe in buying. If it is a good investment and the correct time marketwise, you could take all $10,000 and purchase it.
2	Hold back 25 percent of the money that you were going to invest. If it is a good investment and the correct time marketwise, you could take $7,500 and purchase it. Hold the remaining $2,500 in a money market fund and just continue to see how this investment makes you feel.
3	Hold back 50 percent of the money that you were going to invest. If it is a good investment and the correct time marketwise, you could take $5,000 and purchase it. Hold the remaining $5,000 in a money market fund and just continue to see how this investment makes you feel.
4	Hold back 75 percent of the money that you were going to invest. If it is a good investment and the correct time marketwise, you could take $2,500 and purchase it. Hold the remaining $7,500 in a money market fund and just continue to see how this investment makes you feel.
5	Forget it! You do not feel safe with this investment.

Again, I want to stress that the Fear Factor Scale can be used as a simple touchstone for how you really feel about the investments that you currently own or are considering, as well as, in a modified form, for evaluating how you feel about any purchases you are about to make. In that case, you will consider how comfortable you feel spending on the purchase. If you can't get it at the price at which you feel comfortable, you shouldn't be buying it at this time.

I am not suggesting that you use this scale to replace a financial advisor or professional. But you can use it to help you evaluate your reactions to their advice. Perhaps—just perhaps—if you had had this scale while the market was going down in the year 2000, you might have gotten out before you watched all your money go down the drain. If you didn't suffer that kind of financial setback, you can move ahead without the weight of personal history affecting your decision making. And the Fear Factor Scale will absolutely help you afford your future, too.

Law Number 4

INVEST IN THE KNOWN
BEFORE THE UNKNOWN

Over and over again, I hear the same questions and problems from my readers and television audience. Here's a sample:

- "I don't know what to do—I've lost a lot of my money and I'm sixty-five years old."
- "I don't know what to do—I just got laid off from my job and no one is hiring in my area. Soon I'm going to be totally out of money."
- "I don't know what to do—I want to buy a home but the prices just keep going up."
- "I don't know what to do because interest rates are so low that my interest income will not pay my bills anymore."
- "I don't know what to do about the creditors who keep calling. They're threatening to sue me if I don't pay them, but I don't have the money!"
- "I don't know what to do. Should I sell my stocks because they've gone up a little or just hold on?"

It is as if the words "I don't know what to do" has become a kind of desperate refrain, a bad, out-of-control financial mantra. But then, why would anyone know what to do when almost none of the financial experts agrees with one another about it and are constantly giving conflicting advice? If the experts are confused, how are you supposed to know what to do?

Today, whenever I answer people's questions, I find myself always giving the same advice that I have been giving for years. But even though the advice is the same, the truth is that you confront more economic uncertainty—or what I call the unknowns—than at any time I can remember. I no longer believe that we can predict what will happen in our economy based on past historical data. So my advice for all the many difficult situations you may be facing or face one day basically adds up to this, the fourth law of money: You must invest in the known *before* the unknown.

INVESTING IN THE KNOWN
VERSUS THE UNKNOWN

Law 4 basically says that you must put your money first toward those things that you know you need in life or have an obligation to pay for, such as food, shelter, transportation, debt payments, and your retirement. (Later, I'll say more about the order in which it's best to put your money toward these things.) You must do this *before* you invest in unknown things like a bigger house, investment real estate, or a nonretirement stock market account. To me, this law ties into the Eighth Commandment, against stealing. Why? Because I want you to see that when you invest in the unknown before you invest in the known, you are really stealing from yourself. You're stealing from your safety, your well-being, and your future. You're probably also stealing from your family's safety and well-being. And you're not following the first three laws: you are not telling yourself the truth about your money and your most important needs, you are not facing what you really have, and you are not doing what's right for you.

Now don't get carried away by an immediate reaction against this law. The law does not say that you should never ever invest in the stock market or in the investment real estate market. It says that you must work with your money in a very systematic way so that you are always as well prepared as possible for any unforeseen event that can negatively affect your life. In general, you will put the majority of your money to work in those things that you can most easily foresee and control, what I call the known investments, *before* you venture out with additional sums of money into the wide, increasingly risky unknowns. When you follow the letter of this law, you bring a new sense of security and order to your financial life.

YOUR MONTHLY EXPENSES: THE DIFFERENCE BETWEEN KNOWN AND UNKNOWN

During the course of your lifetime, one of your biggest challenges may be to make sure that you continually have enough money to pay for your monthly expenses. It really is the only reason that you work, isn't it—to make sure you have enough to pay those monthly bills? Some of those expenses, such as taxes, utilities, food, and out-of-pocket medical and dental expenses are ongoing bills, so to speak. They will come, month in and month out, for the rest of your life, whether you rent your home or own it outright, whether you are working or retired. You can't eliminate or retire these expenses—or know for sure how much they will be each month. These are what I call the unknown expenses. And when it comes to unknown expenses you have got to understand that they will always be there in varying amounts for the rest of your life. So, you will always need money to pay for them. Therefore, the best actions to take with unknown expenses is to create enough income-generating investments or savings to pay for them in case the unforeseen—for instance, an illness or a job lay-off, or an unexpected retirement—happens.

But there are also what I call known expenses that you *can* choose to eliminate or retire over time. Retirement saving is one example: once you are retired, the amounts you may be contributing to your IRA or 401(k) will no longer be deducted from your pension check; in a sense then, this is an expense that retires itself. Debt payments are another example; as you get the resources, you can eventually pay off your credit card debt or student loans and never have to deal with those bills again. In many cases, debt payments are for items that you have bought but that were too expensive for you to pay for outright at the time of purchase, so you finance them with a mortgage, a car loan, or even a credit card. Known expenses, such as mortgage and car payments, require fixed amounts that you pay every month for a specific period of time until the debt is paid in full.

IDENTIFYING YOUR BIGGEST KNOWN EXPENSES

Besides ongoing expenses, the highest monthly known expenses that you most likely have are:

- house payment
- car payment
- recreational vehicle or boat payment
- student loan debt payment
- credit/store card payment (depending on your balance)

THE GOAL: ELIMINATE YOUR KNOWN EXPENSES ENTIRELY

The easiest, most foolproof way to make sure you can always pay for your known expenses no matter what unknown event comes your way, is to reduce these known expenses—and ultimately eliminate them altogether. In other words, you want to make it your primary financial goal to eliminate as many as possible of the known expenses of your life. By doing this, you will knowingly be taking actions to reduce the highest mandatory monthly outgo of your money sooner than later—which will be extremely valuable if the unknown happens.

Now that we have talked briefly about unknown and known expenses, let's talk about what the possible known and unknown events of your life could be.

THE POSSIBLE KNOWN EVENTS IN YOUR LIFE

During the course of your life, you will face certain events (whether or not you want to) that could affect your ability to meet your monthly financial obligations. The two most predictable known events that I will talk about here are:

- retirement—yours, or that of your spouse or your life partner
- death—yours, or your spouse's or your life partner's

Planning for These Unknown Events

While it is true that upon your own death you no longer have to pay your bills, the loved ones who you leave behind still need to do so, and your death could make it financially difficult for them. Therefore, you have to plan for this known event, whether you want to or not. Remember: It is not an *if* that you are going to die; it is a *when*. This we know.

The same is true with retirement. Many people feel, think, or hope that they are never going to retire; therefore, they believe they do not have to worry about planning to cover their known expenses with a fixed, lower income because there will always be a paycheck coming in. Yet one day you may change your mind, or you may be forced to retire because of downsizing, age, or an unknown illness. By not wanting to recognize this probability, you will not stop it from happening. Deep down, you know that. In my opinion it is even more important for you to plan knowingly for your retirement than for your death, for *you will be here* to experience your retirement, for better or worse.

THE POSSIBLE UNKNOWN EVENTS

You need to understand and *know* that the main unknown in your financial life—and where most people tend to get in trouble with their money—is when something happens that you are not expecting. A job loss, an accident, a family crisis, an illness (either your own or that of a parent or a child), a death or disability, or an unexpected divorce—each is an unknown event that affects your expenses and finances. When an unknown event does occur, your biggest problem usually will be to know where to get the money you need to pay for your known expenses and your unknown, unanticipated ones until you can become safe and secure again. Keep in mind that your financial world can be shaken or destroyed by very common, unforeseen possibilities. This has always been the case, of course—and in a time of economic and global uncertainty, it is especially true. People who sail through difficulties with relatively little financial harm do so because they have prepared for them. We'll talk about how you can do this throughout the chapter.

START LIVING BY THIS LAW NOW

Because you cannot predict when and where an unknown event is going to hit, it is essential that you start to live by this law right now and that you follow step by step what I am telling you to do. But it is not enough for me just to *tell* you what to do, for you also need to understand *why* you should take certain steps, such as setting up an emergency fund, buying rather than leasing a car, and paying off your home mortgage. So, I'm going to explain to you why you need to put this law into action so that you are prepared if other financial advisors give you conflicting information. Other financial advisors may say, "No, don't set up an emergency fund. Invest that money in the stock market now and take advantage of its upward climb. Or, buy more investment real estate, lease that new car, continue to get yourself more and more in debt, and buy, buy, buy." I want to show you why, in my opinion, debt is the enemy of the security I want you to have and why it's against the laws of money.

Please note that in this chapter, you will find few stories of other people. When it comes to what you actually need to do with your money, you do not need to read anyone else's story—you just need to use your own life as an example. This law comes after Law 3, the most personal law, the law in which you have to do what's right for yourself first and then your money. Law 4, by contrast, is the most impersonal law; it describes the actions that all of us must take. But in order to take action in the rational way you need to, you need to have done the work of telling yourself the truth, of knowing what you have and what you need.

THE FIRST KNOWN STEP

In order to bring your financial life out of the unknown into the known, the first step in your systematic plan must be to make paying off all debt—but *especially* credit card and other consumer debt, including car loans, and personal bank loans—your first priority.

Now, why is getting out of debt so important? Because with this kind of debt, you are paying for your present-day desires at the cost of your future needs. Credit card debt is really a form of bondage to the past. It's a violation of Laws 1 and 2, and it also makes it impossible for you to abide by Law 3. Now I know you may have gotten into credit card debt because you lost your job or got ill and you had no other way to pay expenses except by using your credit card. I understand that and I actually think that is what credit cards should be used for. But the truth is that most people who carry large credit card balances have not lost their jobs or fallen ill or really needed the cash advances. They simply bought things they wanted on credit because they could not afford to pay cash.

You may be one of these people. If so, isn't it true that you just want what you want when you want it and, because of credit cards, you can get what you want?

Like Patrick in the first chapter, most of America is in extreme credit card debt—on average, $9,000 per household at the beginning of 2004. And what is so sad is that most of that money is spent on vacations, meals, electronic equipment, and clothes, which all lose their financial worth as soon as you buy or consume them—and with each payment you consume more and more of your current and future money. Also, the interest on your credit card debt compounds, so you are robbing yourself of money from many paychecks *far* into the future.

Make no mistake about the seriousness of being debt-bound. Credit card debt is an enforceable legal obligation that you carry with you through divorce, illness, and even some kinds of bankruptcy. Do you have credit card debt you cannot afford to pay off today? If so, I don't want you to dwell at length on the past, for that could paralyze you, as I explained in Law 2. But I *do* want you to stop and think about this: Can you remember ever saying to yourself that it is okay to charge an item that you want, because next year you will be making more money and will be able to pay for it in full? If you are like most people, the answer is yes. Yet many people are now *making* more money than the year before and still haven't begun paying off those credit card balances. You may even still be paying just the minimum amount due on your cards each month. The fact is, when most people make more money, their debt doesn't decrease at all. It increases. How about you? Has your debt actually increased as you've earned more?

If the answer to that question is yes, I want you to remember Patrick from Law 1. Like him, when you can't pay your credit card bills in full each month, if the unknown happens and you do not have the money to pay them, you will be filled with fear. And fear, like lies, repels money and is an enemy of wealth. So, let's start right now to learn the keys to getting out of credit card debt.

THE KNOWN KEYS TO GETTING OUT OF CREDIT CARD DEBT

USE YOUR SAVINGS NOW TO PAY OFF DEBT

When interest rates are low, as they have been in recent years, if you have any savings in a certificate of deposit (CD) or a money market fund (MMF) outside your retirement accounts, you should seriously consider using some or all of this money to pay off your high-interest credit card debt. I know, I know—you'll say, "But Suze, my savings is all I have! It's my only security!" But this is a false sense of security. It is like knowing that you have a rowboat full of holes sitting outside of your house in case a flood comes. This boat probably will not stay afloat long enough to get you to where you may need to go. The same is true when you *have* money and you *owe* money. You may feel that you have a safety net, but you do not. What sense does it make to pay more interest on the money you are borrowing than you are getting on your savings?

In truth, if you have $9,000 of credit card debt at an 18 percent annual interest rate and you are keeping $9,000 in a MMF on which you are earning 1 percent a year (1 percent that is *taxable* to you), you are losing over 17 percent a year on your money for that false sense of security. This makes no sense at all. This is one of the reasons you are sinking financially and cannot stay afloat. You are saving money but it may be costing you your financial future.

If you are in that situation—if you have the money to pay off your credit cards—here's what I want you to do. Pay off the cards. Once you've done that, take the entire payment you had been making on your cards (that is, when you were paying the minimum amount due, or slightly more) each month and put that exact amount back into your MMF each month. Within a relatively short period of time, you'll have your savings back— and more. At the same time, you *must* stop charging things you don't need. Try to pay cash for any purchases you now make so you don't add to your debt.

Meanwhile, if an unforeseen crisis happens and you do need extra money before your nest egg is back to its former size, you can take out a cash advance on your now pristine credit card account or on an equity line of credit (we will talk about that in the emergency fund section below). You may have noticed that the interest rate on a cash advance is higher than what you are currently paying on your credit cards. Even if it is slightly higher than the national average on credit cards—it's around 21 percent these days for cash advances, 3 percentage points higher than the credit card rate—you can always transfer your balance (even if it is made up of a cash advance) on that credit card to a new credit card at a lower introductory interest rate if your credit rating is good.

———

What to Do If You Don't Have Savings to Pay Off Your Credit Card Debt

If you have credit card or other consumer debt and you don't have enough savings (outside your retirement accounts) to pay it off in full right now, use the instructions that are in the guidebook at the back of this book for the best way for you to start to pay off credit card debt.

Let's look at the next two keys to getting out of credit card debt sooner rather than later:

PAY MORE THAN THE MINIMUM

The first thing you must do is to always pay more than the minimum required. Credit card companies can be very tricky. They play the unknown against the known very well. They know that you do not usually pay more than they ask of you. They know that you do not really understand how the compounding of the interest rates they charge you, along with the calculation of the minimum payments due, really works. Because they know that you are *not* in the know about this, they can profit handsomely from you. And you do not even know that they are doing this! So you just keep letting them take from you and your future. You become complicit in stealing from yourself. This leads to a serious waste of your money.

YOUR EXERCISE

Consider this scenario:

You have $25,000 of credit card debt and you decide that you will never charge another penny on this card. You pay only the minimum that the credit card company asks you to pay each month. Your interest rate is 18 percent and the minimum payment is just 2 percent of your balance. How long will it take you to pay off this debt in full if you never ever charge another penny?

A. 8 years
B. 22 years
C. 34 years
D. 73 years

And how much will you have paid in interest over that time?

A. $4,000
B. $21,000

C. $52,000

D. $74,000

If you picked D both times, you are correct. You read that right, the answer is D. Now over those 73 years, while you are paying interest on a purchase that you used up or tossed out long ago, do you think one of the known or unknown events that we talked about earlier is bound to happen? Maybe not, but probably yes.

Please note: If you have the national average of $9,000 of debt, in this scenario it still would take you *56 years* to pay it off. That's how far into the future the cost of even a medium-size debt can extend. Doesn't that sound like a prison sentence? Do you see how important it is to free yourself from the chains of debt?

Why Does It Take So Long to Pay Off?

In this example, the minimum payment that is required during the very first month on $25,000 will be $500. As your balance starts to go down, the credit card company readjusts your payment each month; it lowers your minimum payment so that it remains, in this case, just 2 percent of your outstanding balance. Therefore, if you always just pay the minimum that is asked of you, at that interest rate it will take you 73 years to pay it off and you will have paid $74,000 in interest. However, if you were to continue to pay $500 per month (the original minimum requested amount), it would take you only 8 years to pay it off and you would be paying only about $21,500 in interest. Do you see what a big difference that makes?

GET THE LOWEST INTEREST RATE POSSIBLE

The second key way to getting out of credit card debt sooner rather than later is to get the lowest possible interest rate you can. This matters a lot and is something that you really need to know.

YOUR EXERCISE

Let's recalculate the scenario above by assuming that, instead of paying an 18 percent interest rate on this credit card debt, you are paying 5.9 percent. At that lower rate, how long do you think it would take you to pay off that $25,000 if all you ever paid was the 2 percent minimum payment required?

A. 5 years
B. 26 years
C. 43 years
D. 63 years

And how much do you think you would have paid in interest?

A. $3,700
B. $8,000
C. $13,000
D. $25,000

The correct answer in both cases is B: 26 years and $8,000 in interest.

As you can see, getting a lower interest rate makes a big difference, even if all you can afford is the minimum payment each month.

By the way, if you were to continue to pay $500 per month in this scenario, you would pay off this debt in just 5 years and you would have paid only $3,700 in interest. So it is very important to get the lowest possible interest rate and to always pay more than the minimum.

Knowing How to Get the Lowest Interest Rates Possible

The key to getting the lowest interest rates possible on your credit cards as well as on your home mortgage and car loans is this: You have to fall within the range of the highest FICO scores.

You may not even know what a FICO score is, and even if you do know, you probably do not know your actual FICO score. You probably also need to know how you can improve your score and what you have done or are doing that hurts it.

Your FICO Score

A FICO score is a numeric value assigned to your credit habits and history by a company called Fair, Isaac and Company. Every American who has ever used credit now has a FICO score, and all creditors now use them. In the last few years, this score has become one of the most important criteria for evaluating you when you apply for credit. The higher your score, the lower the interest rates you pay on credit cards, mortgages, and car loans. Conversely, the lower your score, the higher the rates you will be forced to pay.

To find out what your FICO score is, log onto the website www.myfico.com. It will cost you $12.95 to get your score. For other ways to learn your FICO score, log on to my website, www.suzeorman.com.

FICO scores are on a scale from 300 to 850, but they are basically divided into six ranges that correspond with interest rates that are issued by main lenders. Those who fall below the sixth range are in what's called the "sub lenders" category. The six

ranges are what you should concentrate on. The FICO score is
now also being used by insurers, employers, and landlords to evaluate applications. From it, they can discern your work history and
whether you pay rent on time, so it helps them decide if they should
take a risk and insure you, hire you, or rent to you. (This can be
seen best on page 129, in the section on mortgages). What you
need to know *now* is that the higher your FICO score, the lower
the interest rate you can get and vice versa. The six ranges are:

720–850
700–719
675–699
620–674
560–619
500–559

A score between 300 and 499 puts you in the "sub lenders"
category.

To be eligible for the lowest interest rate on your credit cards
as well as other loans, you need to have a FICO score that is in
the top range (720–850). If you are below 620, you are (in your
lender's mind) in financial trouble and you will be hit with a seriously high interest rate. Therefore, you need to take steps to
increase your FICO score.

After checking your FICO score, if you would like to figure
out what you should and should not do to raise it, refer to the
pointers I give you in the guidebook.

If your FICO score is really good (720 or above) then you
should be aware that technically you qualify to get the best (the
lowest) interest rates available on money you borrow. If this is
the case and you are paying a high interest rate on your credit
cards, call your credit card company and say that if it does not

lower your interest rate, you will be switching your account. You might want to actually try to get a card with a better rate first and, when you do, make your current card company beat that rate; if it does not, transfer your credit balance to the new account. But before you close down that first account altogether, check in the guidebook to see what hurts a FICO score.

To find the best interest rate on credit cards, log onto www.lendingtree.com or www.bankrate.com.

CREDIT COUNSELING IS AN OPTION

If you doubt that you can tackle your credit card debt on your own, and you feel that you need help, contact a credit counseling service, such as the National Foundation for Credit Counseling (www.nfcc.org or 1-800-388-2227). These people are experienced, helpful, and relatively inexpensive to use (about $12 a month). They may even be able to negotiate a lower rate or a repayment schedule for you.

In years past, using a credit counseling service actually hurt your FICO score, but this is not as true today. The wise people at FICO have realized that people who use a credit counselor want to help themselves and are not trying to avoid paying their bills, so they do not mark down your score as they used to.

A DIFFERENT KIND OF DEBT: WHAT YOU NEED TO KNOW ABOUT YOUR STUDENT LOANS

Student loans are what I often call good debt, for they are an investment you make today in who you want to become tomorrow. Compared to credit card debt, not only are they good for you, they are also comparatively good for your money, since if you qualify, the interest payments you make on them, up to a certain point, are tax deductible, just as home-mortgage interest is. Nevertheless, just like credit card debt, student loans, too, are an enforceable obligation to pay a creditor at a specific time and a specific rate of interest, no matter what happens in your life. And so they too are really a kind of lien on your future security.

Interest rates have come down considerably since the year 2000, and in 2004 if you are currently paying more than about 4 percent interest on your student loans and have never consolidated them before, you might want to consider doing so now to get a lower interest rate. In effect, consolidating means taking all your loans, bundling them into one loan, and getting a new fixed rate. You can also get a longer repayment schedule—although of course I would advise you against doing this; in fact, I would recommend that you take any monthly savings you reap from the lower interest rate and pay off your student loans or (even better) your credit card debt more quickly. To consolidate your student loans, apply online at www.loanconsolidation.ed.gov or call 1-800-557-7392.

New annual interest rates on student loans are set once a year, on July 1. If you are thinking about consolidating at a time when interest rates in general have been falling, depending on your situation and where you are in the calendar year, you might want to wait to see whether the new rates on July 1 will be lower than the current ones. Here's what to do. If you are just a short period of time away—let's say it is February or March—instead of consolidating now, hold off until May 1 and check out the interest rate the government is paying on the 91-day Treasury bill. That's right—the rate on the 91-day Treasury bill is the rate to which student loan rates are tied. (You can check T-bill rates by logging on to www.publicdebt.treas.gov/servlet/OFBills.) There are formulas that govern how loan rates work. In the case of Stafford Loans, for example, you have a few different rate formulas, which are set July 1 of each year. If you are still in school or your loan is still in the grace or deferment period, your rate will be equal to the 91-day T-bill rate plus 1.7 percentage points. If you are out of school and in the repayment period, the rate is the T-bill rate plus 2.3 percentage points. The new PLUS loan rate—for loans that were made after July 1, 1998—is equal to the T-bill rate plus 3.1 percentage points. PLUS loans made between July 1, 1992, and July 1, 1998, are tied to the 52-week T-bill rate plus 3.1 percentage points. PLUS Loans disbursed between July 1987 and July 1992 are also tied to the 52-week T-bill, plus 3.25 percentage points. If doing the math leads you to conclude that the July rates will be lower than the current rates, wait until the new rates are announced, then consolidate. If you think they will stay the same or go higher, don't wait; check the current rate and consider consolidating now.

If you have just graduated and you are still within the grace period—the period during which you do not yet have to pay back the loan—wait until about five weeks *before* your grace period is up to apply for a loan consolidation. That way, you take full advantage of your grace period but still consolidate your payments as soon as possible once it has ended.

PREPARING FOR A JOB LAYOFF OR OTHER INCOME LOSS

As I finished revising this book at the start of 2004, many economists were saying that the economy was starting to turn around. I hope so. But given that you can't be sure what unknowns await you, I want Law 4 to give you a plan of action that will help you how as well as in years to come. Whether the financial analysts, economists, or advisors are correct or not, wouldn't you like to know that your life will go on with the least possible amount of financial disruption, so you can keep what you have and continue to create what you deserve? I can only imagine that the answer to that question is yes. If it is, then your second priority, after paying off your credit card debt, *must* be to prepare for the unexpected loss of a job.

One of the biggest challenges inherent in many unforeseen financial events is the abrupt, unexpected termination of your primary source of income. To prepare for an unexpected job lay-off or illness that does not allow you to work, please take these known actions that follow *now*, before the unforeseen occurs. That way you'll be in a position of power (more about that in Law 5). You don't want to be in a place in which you're flailing about uncertainly while trying to make important decisions.

SET UP AN EMERGENCY FUND

To make sure you are always prepared for the unknown, the first thing you need to do *after* paying off your credit card debt is to establish an emergency fund to pay your monthly living expenses while you're not working. I want you to have at least eight months of cash saved. Yes, that's right: eight whole months of expenses in savings. I no longer believe that the three- to six-month time frame that has been traditionally recommended as a reserve fund is enough. For one thing, because the economy has changed and job layoffs have become more prevalent, the time it takes to find another job is getting longer and longer.

HOW MUCH DO YOU NEED?

In setting up an emergency fund, the first problem you may encounter is not knowing how much it actually costs you per month to live. Suppose you bring home a monthly paycheck of $3,000. By the end of the month, it's all gone. You may think that is how much you need to live each month, but the truth is you spend far more than that. This is why your credit card debt keeps rising. To find out how much you really do spend each month, see "Know Your Expenses" on page 249 of the guidebook.

Another problem you may encounter in preparing for the unknown is that you find it hard to save—and can't imagine setting up an account with eight months worth of expenses in a short amount of time. Well, my friend, if this is the case, the way for you to create an emergency fund is simply to take every extra penny you have, put it into a money market account, and *save it there*. You have to make a decision here. Which means more to you—having a Starbucks coffee this afternoon and going to the movies tonight, or knowing that you and your loved ones will be protected even if you lose your job or get sick? Doing what is right for you—including making sure you'll have what you need in any situation—may mean giving up what you *want* right now to pay for what you could *need* later on. I hope you decide to do this, for you'll be amazed at how much control over your life you will feel with your emergency fund standing behind you.

An Equity Line of Credit and Credit Cards Can Help Temporarily

While you are figuring out how to save for an emergency fund, here are some actions you can take. If you own a home with equity in it, you might want to establish an equity line of credit with the amount that you need to get you through those eight months of expenses—just in case.

Equity is the value of your home above and beyond what you owe to the mortgage company. If your house has appreciated in value since you purchased it, your equity, or cash value, in that home has increased as well. You might be able to use that cash as an emergency fund through an equity line of credit that you arrange for with a bank or mortgage company. If you are eligible, the lender of this equity line of credit will provide you with a checkbook that will let you write checks against the equity in your home. You will pay interest on only the portion of the funds that you actually use. Equity credit is a good backup to have as you build up an actual emergency fund, but it must be kept safe and used only for a situation in which you have a loss of income. To do otherwise would put you in jeopardy and break this law of money.

If you do not own a home or if your home currently has no equity in it—or even if it does—I want you to take another step toward having the money you will need in case of an emergency. Here's what to do. Apply for and take out one or more credit cards with available credit limits that cover the amount that you will need for your eight months of living expenses. If you cannot get credit limits that cover the entire amount, come as close as you can. If the unforeseen happens—if you become ill or lose your job—you can use this credit by taking cash advances. That said, again, *please* do not use the credit limit on these cards to incur debts if you are currently employed. That would be plunging yourself back into the unknown, big time.

The time to set up both an equity line of credit and credit card lines is when you *do* have a job and income is coming in. If you ever do suffer an unforeseen crisis like a job layoff or illness and you are without an income stream, it will be very difficult to set up these credit lines. Do it now.

WHEN TO USE YOUR AVAILABLE
EQUITY LINE OF CREDIT

It is extremely important that you understand the ramifications of using your equity line of credit. When you are in dire straits, conventional financial wisdom would have you use an equity line of credit first. I recommend, however, that you weigh your alternatives very carefully. If you lose your job and your prospects for getting another one really do not look good at all, or if you fall ill and do not have any idea when you will be able to resume working, using an equity line of credit may not be the choice for you.

That's because an equity line of credit is a secured loan—secured with the deed to your home. Credit card debt is unsecured. Now imagine this: You've taken out and used up your entire $10,000 equity line of credit. You have also used up all the cash advances from your credit cards. You're out of money and have tapped all the equity in your home. Guess what? If you cannot make your payments on the equity line of credit, the bank will most likely foreclose on your home. Now what are you going to do? On the other hand, if you take an advance from a credit card and find you can't afford to pay it back, the credit card company cannot take your home from you. They can sue you, of course, but probably will do so only if they think they can get money from you. If they sue you and win, they will put a lien on your home, but they cannot force the *sale* of the home (foreclosure). A lender with an equity line of credit *can* force the sale and foreclosure of your home. So you must give serious thought to that before you quickly tap an equity line of credit.

Nevertheless, remember that cash advances are expensive

ways to get cash. The credit card companies charge you the highest interest rate they can on cash advances—usually on top of a 2 to 4 percent withdrawal fee. You get no grace period with a cash advance, so interest charges start accruing right away. Even so, you need to weigh the risk of losing your home against simply paying a higher rate of interest on a credit card cash advance to get you by. Also, if things turn around for you and you get another job in which you feel secure, you can consider paying back your credit card advances with your equity line of credit.

A JOB LAYOFF AND
VOLUNTARY SEVERANCE PACKAGE

Sometimes the unforeseen doesn't hit you as brutally as it does with a job layoff, where you come in one day and you are history. Sometimes it comes as a choice. Maybe your employer needs to cut back and asks certain employees to volunteer to leave or be severed from their jobs. As an incentive to you to take this offer, your employer usually offers what is known as a severance package. If this happens to you, it is important that you know in advance whether to take it.

This is what you need to consider: When you're offered a severance package, it normally gives you one to two weeks of pay for every year you have worked for a company. When you hear this, you may think, "Well, all right, they're going to give me $30,000 without my having to work for it; that sounds like a good deal. I'll take it." The question is: Will you get the whole $30,000 to put in your pocket? The answer is no. For tax purposes, severance is considered income, just like your paycheck—and in addition to federal, state, and local income taxes, you'll have to pay Social Security and Medicare taxes on that money.

By the time you get your check, you'll be lucky to get $20,000.

Still, if you think you can quickly find another job, this might look like found money to you. Be careful here. You have to understand that, if you are in a recessionary environment or a tight job market in your field, finding another job might not be as easy as you think. You have to run through these possibilities in your mind, along with your financial calculations. What would happen if you could not find another job—an equally good job—for eight months, a year, or a year and a half? What would you do for income once the severance runs out? Are you willing to spend your emergency fund, if you have it in place?

If you're considering taking a voluntary severance package offered by your company, please ask for a complete rundown of everything that's included in the package, especially company-paid health insurance and the right to keep your health insurance at your own expense under COBRA laws. (COBRA, short for the Consolidated Omnibus Budget Reconciliation Act of 1986, guarantees you the right to continue in your former employer's group health plan for up to eighteen months, at your own expense, even if you voluntarily leave a job.) Also ask whether you'll be eligible for unemployment insurance, should you need it. And please test the employment waters before you accept a severance offer.

SHOP FOR HEALTH INSURANCE PACKAGES

While we are discussing the unknowns of job layoffs and down-sizings, I want to urge you to start shopping for health insurance now—*before* you suffer an unforeseen event. This way, you know exactly where to go at that time to get the best deal, and you won't settle under the pressure of a job loss, an illness, or an emergency for whatever you currently have. If you are covered by health insurance at your job, you will almost certainly be offered eighteen months of your current health insurance under COBRA. Yet this insurance can be expensive, because *you* will be paying the whole bill to keep it, as opposed to when you were employed and your employer most likely picked up part of the tab. You need to find out whether there are better deals out there. Start by checking some of the quoting services that provide instant price quotes on health and other kinds of insurance and can connect you with many major insurers.

Even though many people do keep the health insurance their employers offer under COBRA, remember that when you lose your job, you also lose your income, so you have to make every penny count. Knowing the best place to go for the best price on health insurance *before* the unforeseen happens helps you do that.

YOUR RETIREMENT PLANS

When you get laid off or can no longer work because of an illness, and if you do not have an emergency fund or available credit lines set up, you may be tempted to withdraw the money you need to live on from your retirement plans. While this is not a wise idea in the long run, it is understandable. This is what you need to know about drawing on your retirement funds if you're in a financial predicament.

EMERGENCY MONEY FROM A ROTH IRA

If you do not have emergency funds or credit lines and you need money, the first place you should turn to is your Roth IRA. That's because the Roth IRA has an advantage that many other retirement accounts don't have. No matter why you need the money, you can withdraw any or all of your original *contributions* from a Roth IRA at any time, without owing any taxes or tax penalties whatsoever. This is regardless of your age or how long that money has been in there. What you can't touch is any growth or interest that your original contributions have earned; these cannot be taken out tax-free before five years and before you are 59.5 years of age.

Let's say you are 36 years old, and over the past four years you have contributed $11,000 to your Roth IRA and that $11,000 has grown and is now worth $13,000. If you need money desperately, you can take out any or all of the $11,000 without taxes or penalties, and you do not ever have to put it back. You just cannot touch the $2,000 that your contributions earned—the growth of your money—until it has been there for at least five years *and* you are 59.5 years of age or older.

(To qualify to contribute the *full yearly contribution* to a Roth IRA, you cannot have a yearly AGI [Adjusted Gross Income] of more than $95,000 if you are single or $150,000 if you are married and filing jointly.)

Emergency Money from a Traditional Ira or Rollover

If you have a traditional IRA or an IRA rollover you can take money out in any amount you want once a year, to get you by, for up to sixty days without having to pay taxes or penalties. As long as you replace the money you withdrew—putting the exact amount of money you took out back into these IRAs before the sixty-first day from when you withdrew it—you will be just fine.

As for any amount that you took out that you do not redeposit by that sixtieth day, you will owe ordinary income taxes on that amount and, if you are not at least 59.5 years old, a possible 10 percent federal tax penalty as well. Knowing that you have this short-term access to your traditional IRA and IRA rollover might be the fix for the short-term money you need until you figure out what you are going to do.

BORROWING FROM YOUR 401(K) PLAN

When many people get into a financial bind, they take a loan from their 401(k) plan. This loan usually has to be repaid over a five-year period. One major disadvantage of borrowing against your 401(k) plan at most corporations is that if you happen to leave your job or get fired, the money you have not paid back will all come due, payable in most cases in one lump sum within days or weeks after your departure. If you do not have the money to repay the balance of this loan at that time, the unpaid loan amount will be taxed as ordinary income that year. Also, if you are under 55 years of age by the end of the year in which you lost your job, you will also have to pay an additional 10 percent federal tax penalty. Before you take such a loan, you need to know where you are going to get the money to pay it back if such an unforeseen event were to happen. Given this information, you might decide to make paying back this loan sooner rather than later your number one priority.

But knowing that 401(k) loans are due and payable when you are no longer working for that employer is not the only reason to avoid taking a loan against your 401(k)—especially when the markets are low. Another little-known disadvantage of borrowing from your 401(k) is that you will be taxed *twice* on the amount of the loan you take. Say you borrow $4,000 from your 401(k) to pay off your $4,000 credit card debt. The $4,000 you are borrowing is money you contributed to your retirement account before taxes; the money you use to pay back the loan will be aftertax money. Then, when you go to withdraw this same money from your 401(k) later on in life, you will be taxed on it again.

You cannot take the losses of a 401(k) plan off your taxes, so if you go to take a loan from your 401(k) plan while the market is low, meaning you have already suffered a serious financial hit, you may never see the growth of that money come back. In the long run, this makes no financial sense whatsoever.

OTHER KNOWN FORMS OF DEBT TO ELIMINATE: CAR LOANS AND LEASING

I started this chapter by talking about the known expenses in your life. Apart from a mortgage payment, one of the largest of these expenses is typically your car payment.

A car serves not only as transportation. It also sometimes serves as a status symbol—one way you may choose to show the world who you are or want to be financially. And sometimes the only way you can afford to get behind the wheel of this status symbol is by leasing, rather than buying, a car. I have never liked leasing. I will never like it, and no one will ever convince me that it is an intelligent thing to do with money.

When you lease a car, you take on a monthly expense that, in most circumstances, you will continue to have to pay for the rest of your life. Here is why: With leasing, you do not own the car you are driving; you are paying a monthly fee merely to use that automobile for a few years. At the end of the leasing period you either have to give it back or purchase it for a predetermined price—a price that is usually set in such a way that it may make no sense for you to go ahead and make that purchase. That's because these days the leasing companies entice you with a lower monthly fee to draw you in and then they make up their profits with an inflated residual price—the price you would have to pay to buy the car outright—at the end of the lease. So what you normally do after the lease period is up is turn in your leased auto to the dealer and lease another. And then what do you do? You do it again and again—for the rest of your life.

GOOD LUCK GETTING OUT OF A CAR LEASE

Let's say that you are leasing a car when an unforeseen crisis hits, and you find you can no longer make your lease payments. What are you going to do? Even if you give the car back, you are not off the financial hook; you still owe the lease company the remaining money on the lease.

To get out of your lease, here are your options. You can:

- Buy the car outright or finance it.
- Sell it for as much as possible and pay that amount plus any additional amount you may still owe to the lease company.
- Try to find someone to assume the lease obligations.

If you cannot sell your car outright, you may want to try to find someone who will assume your lease payments. However, keep in mind that when a person assumes a lease from you, it *still* does not mean *you* are off the hook! If the new leaser does not make the payments, the lending company will come after *you*. So be careful with whom you make your agreement to assume the lease.

If you decide to sell the car on your own, you still have to come up with the difference between what you owe the lease company and what you sold the car for. And what happens if you do not have that money? You're in trouble again. Therefore, to make sure you don't find yourself short, you need to prepare for this unknown *when you first consider leasing* if money is tight for you at that time. When you have leased your car, see if you can also get approved for what's called a signature loan, for about $10,000. If you have been approved for a car lease, you can usually qualify for this other loan. This loan will give you the backup to help you get through an unforeseen crisis. Here's how:

Let's say, again, you have leased a car and an unforeseen problem happens and you can no longer make the car payments. Before you turn back the car to the dealer or lender, see if you can sell it on your own. The way you can do this is to run an ad to sell your car for the payoff *only*—do not try to escalate the price to make money, for it will not happen. (You want to attract buyers who can solve your problem, not scare them away.) When a potential buyer makes an offer on your car, negotiate the best price you can in a nice manner. Hopefully, you will arrive at a sum that will help you pay off the lender with what you've negotiated plus your signature loan. If you have any portion of the signature loan left over, pay it back to the bank immediately. You have now eliminated a large car payment for forty-eight to sixty months and the lease is closed or, more important, paid as agreed-upon according to the lease's terms.

If you decide just to return the leased car to the leasing company without trying to repay, be aware that there is a big downside. After you return the car, the company may try to sell the car at an auction. Even if the car sells at auction, however, you will still owe the difference between the balance on your lease at that time and the auction proceeds for the car. Sometimes the company even charges you more for penalties and recapture of depreciation. It is probable that your lease company has a used-car lot. The person who runs that used-car lot can go to that auction and buy your car for, say, $4,000. The problem is that you owed $12,000 on the car at the time you had to give it back. So even with the $4,000 from the sale of the car at auction, you still owe $8,000 to the lease company, and now you have no wheels to get around.

In the meantime, the lease company has your car back on its used car lot, and the car is up for sale. The company can probably sell it quickly for $10,000. Between the $8,000 you still owe and the profit the company is collecting on the sale of the car, someone is making out like a bandit, and it is not you. You are still paying for a car that *you* do not even have. Now this is what is known as a bummer.

WHAT ABOUT THE TAX WRITE-OFFS OF LEASING?

I know that some financial experts want you to ignore all the dangers of leasing. They will show you the tax advantages of leasing over buying and why, in your case, you should lease rather than buy. I do not care about the tax advantages for most people. They are not significant compared to your overriding need to know how you are going to handle any unforeseen financial crisis in your life.

Say you are in a car accident or the car happens to get stolen. As we said earlier, the deal you made with your leasing company most likely has you owing more than the car's current market value, which is all your insurance company may reimburse you for. You can buy extra insurance to protect you against this, called *gap insurance,* and maybe your lease deal included it. But do you know for sure?

Many people who lease just love getting those great tax write-offs for the first year and also love how they look driving a fancy car. However, I have watched as they became absolutely clinically depressed after they saw their car being carted away because they could no longer make their lease payment and yet were still responsible for those payments.

BUY YOUR CAR RATHER THAN LEASE IT

Remember, Law 4, Invest in the Known *Before* the Unknown, is here to help you get into the truly desirable situation in which you do not have known monthly expenses to pay the rest of your life. In the case of your car expenses, you can do this by purchasing your car rather than leasing it. Even if that means you have to pay for your car over time, buying is preferable to leasing if your goal is to be debt-free. Why? Because at any time, if you find that you cannot make a car payment to a bank or other lender, you can sell the car. As long as you have made a good deal initially and have treated the auto well, you can usually get close to what it is worth.

AFTER YOU'VE PAID OFF YOUR CAR

If you did buy your car and had to finance it, once you have finally paid it off, I do not want you to let the monthly payment you were making go into the land of the unknown. If you are totally out of credit card debt and have an emergency fund set up, you might want to consider continuing to pay yourself that exact same amount for the next few years, placing it in an account that you know you will use to buy your next vehicle. If you do this, after making payments into your car account for four to five years, you should have saved enough so that you can buy another new used car outright. This is a great thing to do.

Yes, you read that right. A *new used car*. Given that the minute you drive any new car off the lot it goes down in value by at least 20 percent, why not pick up a new used car when you need one, a car that someone else who got into an unknown situation had to give back? This car may be used but it sure is new to you and, in most cases, this would save you a serious sum of money. If you are just barely making it with your money, and you need to buy a new car, this is an important option for you to consider.

PAY FOR REPAIRS; DON'T BUY A NEW CAR

One of the reasons we Americans do not like to keep our cars for very long is that we do not like to pay for repairs. But this does not make good financial sense. Would you rather pay $1,000 a year in repairs on a car, or $5,000 a year on finance payments? If you do buy a reasonably priced used car and it starts to need repairs, you can use the money you have saved by not buying a new car—even a new used car—to pay for those repairs in a pinch. Overall, a far better use of your funds in the long run is to keep a car for as long as you can. Insurance is less and DMV fees may be less. In addition, precisely because an older car invariably shows signs of wear and tear, you will not freak every time it gets a scratch, so repairs of that nature may cost less as well.

Whether you are leasing or have purchased a car, your goal is to own that car outright sooner rather than later, so you eliminate this known expense.

To help you find out how much of a car payment you can afford, use the playing house exercise on page 127, but substitute your car payment for the home payment.

THE LARGEST KNOWN EXPENSE: YOUR HOME

There's no question that a home of your own is one of the linchpins of financial and emotional security: It is probably most people's most valuable, treasured asset. Your mortgage payment is probably also your highest known expense. If you already own a home, once you get to the point where you know you want to stay in your current home for the rest of your life—and you have paid off your credit card debt and set up an emergency fund—I want you to make paying off your mortgage one of your main priorities. We'll discuss that later. First, I need to address the concerns of those people who don't yet own a home or condominium as well as the concerns of people who own their homes but want to purchase larger ones.

BEFORE BUYING A NEW HOME

I believe with all my heart and soul that everyone deserves to be able to buy his or her own home. But the question is, Can you afford the house you want? If sooner or later it turns out you cannot afford the payments, this home that you wanted and saved for and loved can quickly become a source of insecurity and a way for you to get into serious financial trouble. You can get out and stay out of financial home trouble, however, by following what I have to say in this section very carefully. So, let's begin.

I have found that from the point that you first start to fantasize about buying a home or begin thinking about trading up from the house you currently own it's usually about six to eight months before you really take action and do it. So to make sure that your greatest dream of home ownership does not turn into your greatest financial nightmare I want you to do what I call "play house." I will show you what I mean by using the story of Peggy as an example.

Not long ago, I met a young woman named Peggy, a tenth-grade social studies teacher in a public school in California's Silicon Valley. She had been saving up for a down payment on a home of her own for three years while still living with her mother. Even though Peggy had just received a $50,000 inheritance from her grandmother, she wasn't sure she had enough to buy even the smallest livable house in the cheapest neighborhood within driving distance of her school.

At that time, real estate prices in Northern California were out of control—even after the dozens of technology companies in the area, known of course as the home of computer and software start-ups, had hit the skids. Peggy had looked at her budget every which way. Although banks were willing to let her put down as little as 10 percent, and even though many of her friends had done that, she worried that if she made a down payment of any less than 20 percent, she wouldn't be able to make her monthly mortgage payments on her salary. If she waited until she had 20 percent of the price of the home she really wanted, however, she was afraid she'd be her mother's age before she could buy. So she decided to start looking to see if there was a way for her to afford a home comfortably.

When Peggy first started to look at houses, she found two possibilities that appealed to her: a quaint but somewhat dilapidated two-story frame house with a big kitchen and a sunny yard for $500,000, and a well-built, two-bedroom ranch with a tiny yard for $350,000, which she thought she could live with. In both cases, it was a lot of money for what she would be getting, but at least each was possible in her mind. A friend of hers who is a real estate agent had told her that she could certainly afford the $500,000 house, which she really wanted, but Peggy doubted whether this was true. Peggy figured that, with her savings of $15,000, her grandmother's bequest of $50,000, and a gift from her mother of $10,000, she could put down a maximum of $75,000. Not bad. On the $500,000 frame house, that would be a down payment of 15 percent. On the $350,000 one, it would be about 21.5 percent.

THE TRUTH ABOUT DOWN PAYMENTS AND PMI

DOWN PAYMENTS: THE LEAST YOU SHOULD PUT DOWN

These days some mortgage lenders will let you put down as little as zero to 3 percent of the purchase price of a home in order for you to buy it. They will tell you that, as long as you qualify for a mortgage, you can afford to purchase that home. Here is what I have learned over the years about down payments. I believe your minimum down payment should be at least 10 percent. This is because if you do not know how to save for a down payment on a home and are unable to save at least 10 percent of the purchase price, you may find yourself (sooner rather than later) in a situation in which you can barely pay for the mortgage. Even if you may make your mortgage payments, you may not have the money to pay for anything else, including repairs or the utilities for the house. Keep in mind that the less you put down, the more your mortgage payments are going to be.

PMI (PRIVATE MORTGAGE INSURANCE): WHAT IT REALLY COSTS YOU

If you do not put at least 20 percent down, you will have to pay private mortgage insurance (PMI) on your mortgage. PMI, a mandatory requirement when the down payment is less than 20 percent, gives the lender additional protection against the possibility that you will default on the loan. It usually costs about $45 per month per $100,000 of mortgage, or about 0.05 percent of the mortgage balance. Just to give you an example of how expensive PMI can be: On a $200,000 mortgage, that is an additional $90 per month above your mortgage payment, and that $90 is not tax deductible. When you have to pay PMI you may also be required to pay part of the PMI costs up front and the rest each month until you have at least 20 to 22 percent equity in your home. At that time, PMI payments should stop.

GETTING AROUND PMI PAYMENTS

There are at least two ways around PMI: a so-called piggyback loan. This is how it works. Let's say you have 10 percent to put down on a home and therefore you need to borrow 90 percent of the purchase price. The piggyback loan lets you borrow 80 percent of the purchase price from one lender and 10 percent from another lender. When you do this you avoid PMI, but the second loan will be at a higher interest rate. This strategy will also cost you more money each month than if you put down the traditional 20 percent—on top of paying off a bigger balance on a monthly basis. Nevertheless, with housing prices as high as they are, a 20 percent down payment is out of reach for many people.

One other way around PMI that very few people know about is that if you have at least 15 percent to put down, many lenders will let you pay for all your PMI costs up front. So, for instance, on a 30-year mortgage to pay for PMI costs you will have to come up with 2 percent of the mortgage up front. On a 30-year mortgage of $200,000 that is about $4,000. If you do not have the $4,000 to pay up front, however, that money can be rolled into the mortgage loan, which will cost you only an extra $24 a month at an interest rate of 6 percent. In many cases, this option is far cheaper because you will pay an extra $24 a month that is tax deductible rather than $90 in monthly PMI costs that are not tax deductible.

If you have less than 20 percent to put down, ask your mortgage lender to help you calculate which would cost you less money—paying PMI or a piggyback loan or paying for your PMI costs up front.

Now a down payment is not all you need, obviously, to purchase a home: You also need to know if you can afford the monthly payments and all the extras it will take simply to own that home. So many people say to me, "Suze, I have the money to put down and the mortgage payment is equal to my current rent. Doesn't that mean I can afford the home?" The answer to that question is, No. So before we go back to Peggy's story, this is what I want you to understand: *A mortgage payment is not the same as just paying rent.*

—

MISTAKES TO AVOID

The biggest mistake first-time home buyers can make is to assume that if you have been paying $800 a month in rent, you can afford an $800-a-month mortgage. The banks may tell you this is true, but remember that banks like you to borrow money—it's their business and one of the ways they make a profit.

These days more than ever before, just because you qualify for a mortgage doesn't mean that you can afford the monthly payments. It's a sobering fact that 100 percent of the owners of the houses now in foreclosure once qualified for a mortgage. The percentage of American homeowners starting foreclosure or somewhere in the process of foreclosure is at its highest point in thirty years. Not all of these people lost their jobs or suffered other unforeseen calamities. Some of them just discovered too late that they really could not afford the home they'd bought on what they were making.

Why? Because they didn't plan for how much it was really going to cost. Your monthly costs include not only your mortgage, but also property insurance, property taxes, any possible PMI payments, maintenance, and utilities. Note that not only will your utility payments be higher if the home is larger than your current one, but in many cases you will also be responsible for charges such as water, sewer connection, and garbage removal that renters do not ordinarily pay. Remember, as a home owner, you will become financially responsible for maintaining and repairing things out of your own pocket. It's even written into your agreement with your lender in many cases.

In addition to the above costs, if the home has property, you are responsible for the physical upkeep of that property. If you do it yourself, tending a lawn or garden and removing leaves each autumn requires the purchase of equipment; otherwise, you need to budget for the services of someone who can do the work. Some neighborhoods have regulations about what you can plant and have to plant, and some have home associations to which you may owe annual dues for the maintenance and upkeep of anything the association owns in common—pools, fences, outbuildings, road signs, and speed bumps, among other things. If you're on a private road, you may even be responsible, possibly along with your neighbors, for paving and snow removal.

Even the best maintained homes have appliances that wear out and many new home owners discover that there are more repairs than they had expected. If you buy an older house, you could need a new refrigerator, dishwasher, washer and dryer, air-conditioning units or parts, a hot water heater, heating appliances. You could easily spend a couple hundred dollars every weekend as you're just beginning to live in your house just keeping it up. Even just painting a room costs a bundle and if you buy a new home most of its walls will be white, so you may want to add some color when you move in. If you have a fireplace, you have to make sure that the fireplace, flue, and chimney are in good repair and you'll have to buy any wood that you burn. You're also literally responsible for the roof over your head and may need to replace it or repair it, like Patrick in Law 1. At a bare minimum, you need to sock away $100 a month for maintenance.

Also don't forget: if you're moving farther away from your job you may have additional commuting costs, including monthly train or bus fares and parking.

So now that you see what can go wrong and what it really costs you to own a home, let's go back to Peggy and see how this would have played out with her. Peggy needed to put down $75,000—15 percent of the $500,000 home or 21.5 percent of the $350,000 home. Even with that sizeable down payment, she now needs to figure out how much it will cost her every month to own these homes and if she can afford either one. In Peggy's case, her monthly payments on the two homes she liked varied considerably. With the $350,000 ranch, after she put $75,000 down, her mortgage balance would be $275,000; if her mortgage was a 30-year fixed-rate mortgage at a 6 percent interest rate, her mortgage payments would be $1,648 a month. Her property insurance and taxes would come to approximately $600 monthly. Since she would be putting more than 20 percent down, she would not have to pay PMI. With her $100 a month for maintenance and repairs her total monthly payment would be $2,348 a month.

On the $500,000 frame house, Peggy would have to take out a $425,000 mortgage. Because the amount of the mortgage that Peggy would need is above the current amount for what are called conforming loans (these are loan amounts set by agencies called Fannie Mae and Freddie Mac; as of the year 2003, the designated amount is $322,700), she would have to take out what is known as a nonconforming or a jumbo loan. This is usually 0.5 percent more in interest than is a conforming loan. So if this were a 30-year fixed-rate mortgage at a 6.5 percent interest rate, her mortgage payments would be $2,686. She would also have to pay PMI of $212 a month (0.5 percent of her mortgage), for she would not be putting 20 percent down. Her property insurance and taxes would be a little higher on this house—say, approximately $800 a month plus $100 a month for maintenance. Peggy's total monthly payment would be $3,798.

As a "senior" teacher in her school, her annual take-home salary after taxes is $49,000, or about $4,000 a month. It was thus quite obvious to Peggy that the $500,000 home was out of her reach and her realtor friend was wrong.

But could Peggy really afford even the other home? To find out, I asked her to do another exercise—one that I want you to do before you actually buy a first or a larger home.

PLAY HOUSE—THE ONLY WAY TO KNOW IF YOU CAN AFFORD THE HOUSE YOU WANT

Before you commit to purchasing a home, open up a brand-new savings account. Remember, this is something you want to do well *before* you are really serious about buying a home. Set a date once a month—for instance, the 15th. For the next six months, on that date, I want you to deposit into your new account the exact difference between what your current housing costs (rent, or the total payments you are making on the home you currently own) and the amount you project you will have to pay on your new home.

For example, let's say that you are renting and it costs you $1,500 a month to rent. The house you want to buy will cost you $3,500 a month (including mortgage payment, PMI, property insurance, taxes, utilities, and maintenance). You must deposit the difference between the two ($3,500 – $1,500, or $2,000 a month) into the new savings account, no later than the date you set.

Or, say that you currently own a home and want to buy a bigger home. Your current total monthly payments, come to $3,000, and your new home will cost you $6,200 a month. To play house, you must deposit the difference between the two ($6,200 – $3,000, or $3,200 a month) into a savings account no later than the date you set.

These examples feature the minimum costs. They don't include all the expenses mentioned on page 124, such as lawn maintenance and snow removal. So, if you really want to do a thorough job, you should also figure out which of those other expenses you will have to pay and how much they will cost you.

After doing this for six months, evaluate how making those higher payments—as in playing house—has affected your lifestyle. If you've made all the payments comfortably and on time, you know that you can truly afford this particular home right now. Better yet, you have already accumulated funds to put toward increasing your down payment, helping you with moving costs or closing costs, or even doing a few small renovations on the new home!

If, on the other hand, you missed payments or were late in making any, you cannot afford the house you were thinking about buying quite yet. Instead, look to see what monthly payment would have been comfortable for you, and try that. Maybe the solution is to consider a smaller house or a larger down payment. Nevertheless, you may just have to wait until your finances improve. The good news is that you now know how much you realistically can afford at this time *without* having lost any money in finding out. You should also have a nice sum of money in your savings account that will help you achieve your future goals.

Playing house is a way of trying new financial situations on for size. You can also use it to help you decide if you can afford a car, a boat, or any large known expense that requires a monthly payment.

By the way, Peggy put away the $2,348 she needed for her smaller home every single month, on time. She bought it once she knew she could afford it.

The Next Step—Get The Lowest Interest Rate Possible

When you apply for your mortgage, you will be quoted an interest rate. Obviously, the higher the interest rate, the more your payments will be. Have you ever wondered how that interest rate is determined? Has your brother or a friend gotten a lower inter-est rate than you even though you both applied at the same time for home loans? The interest rate on all home loans, or any loan for that matter, is directly determined by three numbers known as your FICO score. FICO is a company that was formed many years ago that uses all the information on your credit reports to tabulate and assign you a credit score called a FICO score. While you are playing house—and long before you apply for a mort-gage—be sure to find out your FICO score, if you haven't already done so. (To learn how to do this, see page 99.) The interest rate you get on your mortgage will be directly related to your FICO score. Please note that as the FICO score ranges (listed below) go down, the interest rate you may have to pay goes up.

For example, if on October 8, 2003, you had applied for a 30-year mortgage of under $300,700, here are the six FICO ranges and the interest rates you most likely could get.

720–850	5.753%
700–719	5.875%
675–699	6.416%
620–674	7.566%
560–619	8.531%
500–559	9.289%

Notice that if your FICO score falls in the range of 500–559, it could cost you more than 3.5 percentage points more in inter-est than if your FICO score fell in the best range. And as you can see on the chart, that can be a difference of about $600 a month on a $275,000 mortgage.

Why is this important for you to know? Let's say that your FICO score is 619. If you were applying for a mortgage and the above interest rates were in effect at that time, you would have to pay an interest rate of 8.531 percent. Given this, you might be better off waiting to apply for a mortgage while you take the necessary steps to improve your FICO score. Raising your score by just a few points would put you into the next range, where your interest rate would be 7.566 percent. Remember: the higher your FICO score the lower your interest rate.

Let's look at Peggy's case again. Her FICO score would make quite a difference if the interest rates that we cited above were in effect when she applied for her mortgage of $275,000.

FICO SCORE	INTEREST RATE	MONTHLY PAYMENT ($275,000 30-YEAR FIXED RATE)	TOTAL INTEREST PAID
720–850	5.753	$1,605	$302,926
700–719	5.875	$1,627	$310,812
675–699	6.416	$1,723	$345,288
620–674	7.566	$1,935	$421,702
560–619	8.531	$2,121	$488,400
500–559	9.289	$2,279	$542,248

That is almost a $674 monthly difference from the best FICO range to the worst and over $239,000 in interest paid over the life of the loan. So you see, again, why I stress the importance of knowing what your FICO score is. (To learn how to raise your FICO score, see the guidebook.)

When you play house, you might also want to play with the concept of what raising your FICO score would do to allow you to be able more easily to make those monthly payments, for it is a good thing to know.

———

Home Buying: One of the Best-Known Investments

Real estate can be one of the best investments you ever make, especially if you are looking for a primary residence. Let me show you why, financially speaking.

In this example, you buy a home for $100,000 and you put down 20 percent, or $20,000. (Now, I know that most homes are more than that, but let's just use this number to keep it simple. It works the same way with a $500,000 home, a $1,000,000 home, or more.) Most homes appreciate 4 to 5 percent a year in normal markets. Thus, a $100,000 home that appreciates 4 percent rises in value by $4,000 in one year. But it's not $4,000 on $100,000, because you invested only $20,000. It's $4,000 on a *$20,000* investment, which is a 20 percent return on your money.

In theory, the less you put down on real estate, the more money you make on that investment when you sell it at a profit. Think about it, if you had put down only $10,000 on that piece of real estate, you would now have had a 40 percent return on your money for that year ($4,000 of appreciation in value is 40 percent of your $10,000 down payment).

That said, however, it's not just about the return you get on your money when you buy real estate. (And, remember, any investment can go up *or* down in value). It is also about the fact that a primary residence is your *home*. This is where you live, which is very hard to put a price tag on. You certainly don't want to lose it and, as we've said, your mortgage payment is most likely the highest monthly known expense that you will ever have. So don't forget that the less you put down, the more your monthly mortgage payment is going to be.

PAY OFF YOUR MORTGAGE EARLY

Once you have purchased a home you know you can afford *and* you know that you are going to stay in that home for the rest of your life, I want you to start paying off your mortgage early. Many financial advisors and tax planners will tell you, "Don't pay off your home—that is the only tax write-off you have." They are right about the write-off, but ask yourself this: Would you rather have a tax write-off or a home, no matter what unknowns may come your way?

The heart of Law 4 is that you have to be prepared for the unknowns of life, and that means having enough money to meet your expenses each and every month even if you have no earned income coming in. If you lose your job because of job layoffs or because of an illness, or even if you have voluntarily retired, where are you going to get the money to pay your largest bill of all—your mortgage? And your mortgage is not just a bill. It is a payment that lets you have that roof over your head. If you cannot make that payment, where will you live? Uncle Sam will not extend a new set of living quarters to you. You cannot live in a tax return. You cannot live in a stock certificate. You live in your home. That's why, at all times, you have to know where you are going to get the money to pay the mortgage on your primary residence if the unforeseen were to happen.

If you do not have an emergency fund and if you are already maxed out on your credit cards and lines of credit, you have to think about this seriously. Who cares about the tax write-off? Who cares about the leverage? I care that you have a roof over your head, over your soul, over your being. So I want you to go from the unknown to the known in this area of your life. Make it a known goal to own your home outright sooner rather than later—as soon as you know that the home you are living in is the one you want to keep forever.

RETIRED AND ON A FIXED INCOME? OWN YOUR HOME!

There is one more reason that I want you to pay off your mortgage early if you know you are in a home that you are going to stay in, especially for those who are on a fixed income budget.

With interest rates still low in 2004, it is very hard for people on a fixed income or in retirement to earn enough interest on their savings to pay their known expenses. Low rates may be great for home buyers, but eventually they, too, will be on fixed incomes. This is another reason that I want you to pay off the mortgage on your home sooner rather than later. As you get older, if you do not have the income source to make those payments, you could be in terrible trouble.

As you get on in the years of your mortgage, your payments are made up of more principal than interest. Paying off your mortgage can help you as you start to age because the tax write-off at that point is less advantageous.

Let's say you took out a 30-year mortgage for $200,000 at 6.5 percent. Your mortgage payments are $1,264 a month. Let's say, too, that now you have to retire because of a medical condition and you have ten years left on the mortgage. Interest rates on CDs, bonds, and Treasurys are so low that you have very little idea how to get a decent income. You lost 50 percent of the money that you had in your 401(k) plan in the stock market; your company is no longer paying your health insurance premiums; and the costs of everything have gone up tremendously. You do not know how to make your monthly payments on all your bills. You have $200,000 outside of a retirement account in a CD that is about to mature and is earning just 2 percent interest, or $4,000 a year.

You have about $111,000 left on your mortgage, but your monthly payments are still $1,264 a month—identical to what they were when your mortgage balance was $200,000. You are in the 27 percent tax bracket, so your interest write-off in that twentieth year (the reason that you never paid off the mortgage in the first place) amounts to about $2,000 a year and will decrease rapidly from this point on. Your tax savings in year 25 will only be about a $1,236 a year, but you will still be paying the same amount a month ($15,168 a year), just to save that money.

What should you do? The answer in this case is simple, for it makes no sense to let your money sit in a CD earning $4,000 in interest a year—*taxable* interest—when that is less than what you pay in four months of mortgage payments. Even if you include the tax write-off, you are still losing about $10,000 a year, which is a serious waste of money. Take $111,000 out of the $200,000 from your maturing CD and pay off your mortgage. It is that simple. Now you will have reduced your monthly expenses by $1,265 a month.

HOW TO PAY OFF YOUR MORTGAGE EARLY

One of the best ways to pay off your mortgage early is to make just one extra mortgage payment a year. If you are currently paying 6 percent on your mortgage, one extra mortgage payment a year can change a 30-year mortgage into a 24.7-year mortgage. Similarly, it can turn a 15-year into a 13.3-year mortgage.

Reducing your current mortgage is becoming very popular, so the banks have jumped on the bandwagon and started to send out offers to their borrowers saying that a 30-year mortgage can be shortened by 5.3 years by simply switching from a monthly payment schedule to a biweekly one. If you want to do this, some banks say, all it will cost you is $350 as a one-time set-up fee plus $5 a month. Please note, however, that paying according to this biweekly schedule accomplishes exactly the same thing as your taking it upon yourself to pay just one extra mortgage payment every year. I think it is a serious waste of money to pay more to accomplish something that you can do on your own; I would prefer that you do it on your own and save that chunk of money for yourself or your home. However, if you are not disciplined and feel you will not consistently make that extra mortgage payment every year and you want to be sure that your home will be paid off early, by all means use the aid of the bank.

If you want to see how long it will take you to pay off your mortgage if you make an extra payment every year, go to suze-orman.com and check out the mortgage calculators I have there for you in the Resource section.

REFINANCING: HOW TO DO IT WISELY

With interest rates still low in 2004, perhaps you are refinancing your home and taking equity out as you do so. This may seem like a great idea, but in the long run, if you are using that money just to buy things that you do not really need, or if this money is just sitting in a money market account or a CD, or if you are also taking equity out and/or extending the mortgage term by refinancing, this is not a wise use of your funds. And it could really backfire on you if an unforeseen crisis happens. The goal is to get rid of your known expenses as quickly as possible, so nothing unknown can throw you—*not* to increase them.

You do not want to fall into the very common mistake of making payments on your 30-year mortgage for five or ten years and then, when you refinance at a lower rate, taking more money out and adding five or ten years back onto the life of your mortgage. You *should* be looking to refinance if you can get a lower rate, but you should also be looking to reduce the number of years you have left on your mortgage. You also want to make sure you will stay in the house long enough to recapture the costs of the closing. You may have already refinanced a number of times, but it may make sense to do it again if you improved your FICO score (page 266) meaning you would now qualify for a lower interest rate, or interest rates have gone down even further from when you last refinanced. Here's a way to tell whether or not it makes sense for you to refinance: First, unless your situation has changed, you must always keep the length of the mortgage equal or less than what you already have. next, let's say your current mortgage payment is $2000 a month. If you refinance, your new mortgage payment will be $1900. That is a $100 a month savings.

When refinancing, however, you will always pay closing costs, fees appraisals, and other costs. You have to total up the entire amount of money that it will cost you to refinance. Let's say, in this case, it is $6000. You then divide the amount that it will cost you to refinance $6000 by the amount you will be saving monthly ($100), which equals 60. That number stands for how many months it will take you to recoup the closing costs. If you know that you will be staying in this house for at least another 60 months, refinance. If not, do not refinance; it is not worth it.

When refinancing (or financing for the first time), always keep in mind that interest rates on a 15-year loan are about half a percent less than on a 30-year loan. So the rule of thumb is: the shorter the loan, the less it costs. If a 15-year loan is too expensive for you, you might want to look into a 20-year mortgage rather than a 30-year. For every $100,000 of your mortgage at a 6 percent rate, a 20-year mortgage is about $120 more per month than a 30-year mortgage. Chances are, you may be able to finance the difference in your monthly payments with what you are saving because of your new, lower interest rate. That way, you'll own your house ten years earlier at about the same monthly cost to you. That's a good deal.

As I mentioned above, many financial advisors and tax people will tell you that paying off your mortgage early and owning your home outright is the wrong thing for you to do with your money. But I ask you to remember Law 3, which says, people First, Then Money, Then Things. In the long run, if you are just getting by financially, it does not make sense to listen to tax people about your mortgage payments.

———

PLEASE—BECOME MORTGAGE-FREE SOONER RATHER THAN LATER

In 2000, the ABC-TV show *Who Wants to Be a Millionaire,* was at the top of the Nielsen ratings. A contestant named Bob got the question: "Suze Orman writes books about which topic?" Well, of course, he had to use one of his lifelines, but thank goodness the audience knew the answer, finance, and he went along with them. He went on to win a million dollars.

At the time I was a financial contributor for *Today,* which booked Bob a few days later on the show to ask me questions. He asked me, "What should I do with the money I just made?" After I told him to go buy my books (since he had not known who I was), I told him to pay off the mortgage on his home.

After the show was over, I cannot tell you the number of

emails that I got. "What is wrong with you, Suze?" they said. "How could you tell him to pay off his home? All he has to do is take that money and put it in the stock market and he will be a multimillionaire." "That was the worst financial advice I have ever heard. What is wrong with NBC for letting you tell America to pay off their homes? Bob should put his money in technology stocks." That was in March 2000, at the height of the bull market. Let's just hope that Bob listened to me, because it would be very sad if he lost all that money and still had to worry about his known mortgage payments.

THE STOCK MARKET

PAST PERFORMANCE IS NO LONGER AN INDICATOR OF THE FUTURE

I want to tell you here what you need to know about investments and how they currently work. But first I want to say again, as I did at the beginning of this chapter, that the reason this fourth law of money is more important than ever before is that, in my opinion, the financial future may not repeat the past. In particular, nobody can look to the investment past—the past that took place before the corporate scandals, before the mutual fund debacles, before the New York Stock Exchange salary scandals, and before China became a part of the stock market equation, and especially before the events of 9/11—and tell you where the stock market or the economy or the world is going from here. Please keep that in mind as you read this section.

———

TRUST IN YOUR OWN INVESTMENT ADVICE

Given all that has happened since the start of the new millennium, do you feel that there's hardly anyone you can trust to tell you the truth about your money? In my opinion—and I have always believed this—the key to doing well with your investments is to trust yourself more than you trust anyone else. You may believe that you do not have the wherewithal to understand the financial markets. Or you may believe that you need professional financial help to get you to where you want to go with your money. I am here to tell you that you do have what it takes, and I want to ask you to stop thinking that way. Although there may be times when you will want to use a financial advisor—to help you decide whether you need a will or a trust, for example, or to help you plan the safe deployment of a large inheritance—you still must remain totally involved in the decision making. This is your life and your money. Remember what we discussed in depth in the third law: why you have to do what's right for *you* before you do what's right for your money? The truth is, nobody will ever know as much about who you are or care as much about your money as you yourself do.

If you have a financial advisor, please ask yourself these questions about him or her: Where was he or she in the years 2000–2002? I want you to be honest with yourself (truth creates money, remember?). In the beginning of the year 2000—if and when you had money invested in the stock market and still had a very nice profit on the books—did your advisor tell you to get out or even to safeguard some of your gains? Did your advisor or any of the financial institutions or commentators you rely on actually guide you to protect your hard-earned savings? If you are of retirement age or have parents who are of retirement age and who couldn't afford to lose money, were the professionals willing and able to help you protect your retirement money, so that your quality of life was not adversely affected? Maybe they helped, but probably they did not. So the advice in this section is for you. I want *you* to use it to keep what you have and to create more, not less.

––––

Are You Ready to Retire? Your Guidelines

Sooner or later you are going to have to retire. You may be nowhere near that date as you are reading this, but this exercise will be good for you to try anyhow so that you're prepared when that retirement day does come. The key thing is to make sure you have enough money to be able to enjoy retirement. So to prepare for this known event the first thing that I want you to do is to review Laws 2 and 3 because they will help you decide what to do with your investments if you ever feel you need to make a change. (Please also use the guidebook before you take any action.)

––––

Retirement Money That Does Not Belong in the Stock Market

To make sure that you are not caught off guard when your expected retirement date arrives I want you to start this process by looking at one of the known facts of your life. Do you have at least five years or longer before you need the money that you have invested in the stock market, either in retirement accounts or in your regular stock accounts? If the answer to that question is no—if you don't have that many years—then any money that you will need for your retirement does not belong in the stock market now. Why? You may need to use this money to generate income when you are about to retire. Because of this, you can't afford to risk it. The world at large as well as your own personal world contains too many uncertainties and unknowns to take a chance. Are you going to suffer a job layoff before you retire? Might you get ill? Are you going to have an unexpected death in the family or a divorce? Will the country enter another recession? Is there more corporate fraud about to be exposed? Are we going to be attacked again on our homeland? If *any* of these unknowns were to happen and you and your money did not have time to recover from the consequences, then you could be in financial trouble.

If time is not on your side, you must figure out the amount you will need to cover your living expenses in retirement, then bite the bullet and come out of the market with that amount. You have to go from the *unknowns* of life to *know*ing what you have and keeping it safe and secure.

Let me give you a real-life example of how important this is.

IS TIME ON YOUR SIDE?

If you had been invested in the market during the years 1973 and 1974, you would have seen the NASDAQ stock index lose more than 59 percent of its value. Let's say that in 1972 you knew that you were going to retire in five to ten years. At that time, you knew you would need every cent of your money to generate income for you to live on. You thought you had plenty of time to accumulate capital, so you decided to leave this money right where it was, which happened to be mostly in NASDAQ stocks.

Fact: If you were invested there at that time and thus suffered heavy losses in 1973–1974, it could have taken you at least twelve years (depending on the particular stocks you had) *just to break even*—in other words, for your principal to return to 1972 levels. Forget about any gain!

"But," you say, "things move so much faster now, Suze. Maybe it would not take that much time to come back today." At the start of 2004, even though the NASDAQ has increased 77 percent from its low, it is still down 61 percent from its high in 2000—which is essentially the same percentage loss as in 1973–1974, which took twelve years just to get back even. So let's do the math.

Let's assume that in 2000 you still had seven years until you knew you were going to need your money to retire. Here you are in 2004 with four years left until you no longer have your job and paycheck. Your portfolio is down by 61 percent. What are the chances that you will have all your money back by the time you retire? Very slim, my friend.

HOW MUCH MONEY DO YOU NEED FOR RETIREMENT?

When you are a few years away from retirement, one of the most important things you need to do is figure out just how much money you will need to keep safe and sound in order to generate income to live on. In other words, you need to know what your retirement expenses and your retirement income are likely to be, so that you know exactly how much of your capital you will need to keep out of the stock market and out of harm's way. Let's do that and then, if you have money left over, I'll help you reexamine your asset allocation mix.

ESTIMATING YOUR KNOWN
RETIREMENT EXPENSES

Please go to the "My Monthly Expenses" (page 251) and "My Expected Retirement Expenses" (page 275) worksheets I've provided in the guidebook and use them to figure out exactly how much it is going to cost you (or is costing you now, if you're already retired) to live month in and month out.

When you stop working, a few of your expenses might decrease—you won't have to pay for transportation to get to work, buy office clothes, or eat out as often, for example—but other expenses might go up. If you have time on your hands, you might spend more money on traveling, visiting the kids or calling them on the phone, or playing golf. So, as you fill in the worksheets, think about your life after retirement in a very truthful, realistic way.

Be rigorously honest with yourself. Keep in mind the lesson of Law 1: truth creates money, lies destroy it. Also keep in mind that you must look at what you have *now*, not at what you once had, what you lost, or what you believe that you might make back in the future. Remember, too, that you must do what is right for you *before* you do what is right for your money. This exercise will take time and thought, but if you are going to be comfortable in your retirement, you have to plan. In order to plan, it is absolutely essential that you know how much money you will actually need to have.

COMPARING YOUR KNOWN
RETIREMENT EXPENSES WITH
YOUR KNOWN RETIREMENT INCOME

Once you know the monthly amount of money that you will need in order to enjoy your retirement, you need to look at the amount of income that you know will come in month in and month out, no matter what. This includes your Social Security income, your pension, and any annuities you may have—but not a windfall payment, like a recent one-time tax refund. Use the "My Expected Yearly Retirement Income" worksheet in the guidebook to calculate this amount.

Now subtract your guaranteed income from your anticipated expenses. Let's say that your expenses are $3,000 a month and that between Social Security payments and your retirement fund you have $2,300 a month coming in. This leaves you $700 a month short of meeting your expenses.

SAFEGUARDING YOUR RETIREMENT MONEY FOR ADDITIONAL INCOME

Now let's look at your liquid assets—not just the liquid assets in your retirement accounts, but all your liquid assets. This is where our asset allocation model will come in.

Take the amount that you will need coming in and multiply it by 12 to give you the yearly amount (before taxes) by which you are short. In our example, the $700 shortfall × 12 makes $8,400 a year. Now multiply this number—the yearly income you need—by 20. This will give you the amount of money that you will need to keep yourself safe and sound—meaning that you will keep it invested in bonds or other safe investments generating at least 5 percent a year—to generate income to make up your income deficit.

In our example above, $8,400 × 20 = $168,000. So $168,000 is the least amount of the money that needs to be invested, very safely, to give a 5 percent return. If you had, let's say, $300,000 in all your accounts, including your retirement accounts, then at least $168,000 of that money would need to be put in a place where absolutely nothing could happen to it, so that you would always have that money to generate the income you know you will need.

If you want it to be extra safe and sound, you can and should put more than that amount into very safe investments to account for inflation, which could increase your expenses.

INVESTING A PERCENTAGE OF YOUR REMAINING RETIREMENT ASSETS FOR GROWTH

In the example above, based on total liquid assets of $300,000, your retirement asset allocation mix would be 56 percent in safe bonds and 44 percent elsewhere. This means putting that 44 percent anywhere else you wanted, including in stocks and mutual funds that will let your money continue to grow—as long as you know, without a shadow of a doubt, that you will not have to touch that money for at least the next five to ten years. If all you had in your accounts was $200,000, you would still need $168,000 kept safe and sound, and so your asset allocation mix would be 84 percent invested in safe bonds and 16 percent in whatever else you wanted. If all you had was $168,000 in your accounts, then 100 percent of your assets would have to be kept safe.

This leads me to a crucial point: When you have five or fewer years until retirement, it is not your age but rather how much you need to live on and how much money you currently have that determines your personal retirement asset allocation mix. It's not your chronological age but your financial needs that you must pay attention to. As you can see, there is no one model that works for everyone; the principle of generating enough income so that you can cover your expenses does.

STOCK MARKET DIVERSIFICATION

For any money that you have decided can stay in the stock market for growth and that you have decided to invest in individual stocks rather than mutual funds, it is mandatory that you have *no more than* 4 percent of it in any one stock. Do not repeat the mistakes of those Enron and WorldCom employees who had all or most of their retirement money in their company stock. You may have all the faith in the world in the company that you work for, or you may have an emotional attachment to a stock you purchased or inherited from your parents, but please don't fail to diversify your holdings. In the case of a portfolio made up of individual stocks, this is the rule: You *must* have at least twenty-five stocks, with no more than 4 percent of your funds in any one stock, to make up your stock portfolio. If you cannot do this, consider buying a no-load mutual fund or an exchange-traded fund (ETF) instead.

INVESTMENTS THAT ARE CONSIDERED "SAFE"

In this economic environment, where interest rates are low, you might want to look at investing any money you need to keep safe and sound in the following vehicles.

- Treasury notes and bonds
- Series I bonds
- Series EE bonds
- Ginny Maes
- CDs
- Single-premium deferred annuities that guarantee an interest rate for the entire time the surrender charge is in force.

✦ Insured municipal bonds (outside of a retirement account only).

For more information on these investments, please consult my other books or go to my website, suzeorman.com, and find the information that you need.

Please do not consider investing in intermediate or long-term bond funds under any circumstances. Please don't invest in individual corporate bonds or preferred stock unless you are a very sophisticated investor.

What You Need to Know About Interest Rates and the Fed Fund's Rate

What if you're retired? What if you're older? What if it's driving you nuts to be invested in the stock market? What has the lowering of the fed fund's rate done to you? When this rate goes down, other interest rates on CDs, money market funds, and savings accounts also tend to go down. It can act like a domino effect.

Note: Even if you are not close to retiring, you should read this section for your parents. And it is important that you know what happens to your and their future income when interest rates are lowered, as well as when they are raised.

Here, in a chapter that deals with investing in the known rather than the unknown, we are primarily going to deal with when interest rates are lowered. As of the beginning of 2004, interest rates are the lowest they have been in forty years, at 1 percent.

WHAT HAPPENS WHEN THE FED LOWERS THE RATE?

When the fed fund's rate (what banks charge each other for overnight loans) is lowered, even though there is no direct correlation, what tends to happen in the other income sectors of the financial markets is:

- ✦ The interest rates on money market funds tend to go lower.
- ✦ The interest rates on certificates of deposits tend to go lower.
- ✦ The interest rates on municipal bonds, on Treasuries, or on any instrument that gives interest income tend to go lower.

FED FUNDS RATES AFFECT FIXED INCOMES

The problem with a drop in the fed's rate typically starts for you when you have a bond or a CD that is maturing, or coming due, and you cannot get an interest rate that matches the one you've gotten used to and perhaps depend upon. Say, for instance, that years ago you purchased a $100,000 CD that was giving you 8 percent a year, or $8,000 annual income. Now that CD has matured and you take that $100,000 and all you can get is 4 percent on a five-year CD, or $4,000 a year of income. That is a decrease of 50 percent of your income.

This example shows how, if interest rates stay low shortly before or during your retirement, you *could* be in a financial dilemma. That is why reducing your known expenses really can help prepare for the unknown.

INVESTING IN THE STOCK MARKET
WHEN TIME IS ON YOUR SIDE

What if you are in the market and you know you have at least twenty, thirty, or even forty years until you need your money? In that case, you are in luck. When time is on your side, then even when the markets are down—in fact, especially when they are down—the habit of investing consistently, month in and month out through your retirement account, such as a 401(k), can pave the road to wealth. If you start now and are consistent, you will probably have the very best investment years of your entire life. This can be true even given the unknowns that can occur, assuming that you have taken care of other unknowns such as your credit card debt and your emergency fund.

Let's look at how this works by taking the knowns into consideration. You are young. You know that when you put money into a retirement account such as a 401(k) plan, you do not pay income taxes on the amount that you contribute, so you will save yourself money in taxes for now. You know you are not going to touch this money until you are older because of the penalties for early withdrawal. You are not sure what to invest your 401(k) in, so you indicate you want an index fund within your retirement account that just buys the whole market.

What will happen to this index fund if the market goes up right away? The more the market goes up, the more expensive the shares of this index fund become for you to buy with the automatic monthly contributions from your paycheck you've set up. The more expensive the shares are, the fewer shares you actually can buy each month, and the less money you will make.

The reverse of this process is also true: The more the market goes down, the less expensive the shares of this index fund become for you to buy each month. The less expensive the shares, the more shares you actually can buy with your monthly contribution to your retirement account. The more shares you have when the market does go back up and the price of the shares of the index fund also go up, the more money will you make.

If you are of an age when you know that time is on your side, now is the time to start investing. And please don't stop investing when the markets come down. If you're young, now is the time to contribute the maximum to your 401(k) plans. Find out whether you are eligible to contribute the maximum to a Roth IRA at the same time, for, if you qualify, you can have both a 401(k) and a Roth. You can also have both a self-employed plan and a Roth, if you qualify. Take advantage of these opportunities and go for it.

No matter what your age, however, you have to know whether your stomach and spirit can take the unknowns of investing. Please remain aware of all the other laws in this book, especially Laws 2 and 3, about knowing what you have and knowing what's right for you.

Do Not Be an All-or-Nothing Investor

One thing that you should know about the stock market is that it almost never goes straight up or straight down. The 1990s, in which the market climbed to dizzying heights over the course of about six years, was a remarkable exception and one that, in my opinion, we are not very likely to see again in our lifetimes.

In fact, for the foreseeable future, I believe that we are likely to see short- or medium-term rallies, in which stocks go up for a year or two or three, followed by declines that could easily leave us right back where we were in October 2002. This may or may not happen, but keep in mind that, if you do start to see this happening, don't just let it knock you for a loop as it did to many people during these past few years. You can take some action to help yourself. Remember to keep track of your time frame for when you will need retirement money and how much. Remember to keep track of how you are feeling about your investments, and whether they are causing you fear. Remember to do what is right for you and to invest in the known before the unknown. And remember not to be an all-or-nothing investor.

When people do not know what to do, many tend to do nothing. That is why—like Sam in Law 2—so many people simply watched their stocks go up by as much as 200 percent from the price at which they bought them and then watched them go back down again, sometimes to the point where they lost all their money. Maybe you did this too. One of the biggest mistakes that you might have made as an investor during these past few years is that you became what is known as an all-or-nothing investor.

Let me ask you to consider this. When you are confused, instead of doing nothing at all or doing everything all at once, take a more measured stance. If a stock or mutual fund you own goes up 20 percent and you still are not sure of the direction the investment is taking, or if you still do not know what to do, sell another 20 percent and bank that. If the stock goes down 20 percent, take the same approach—sell 20 percent. But *stay in touch with your money*. You are the one who has the power. And you can exercise that power rationally and intelligently whether the market is going up or down. You *can* know what to do. With this practice, I'm introducing you to Law 5, about which you'll learn much more in the next chapter: Your money has no power of its own. All its power flows through you. You must protect it, and with it, your comfortable future.

SHOULD YOU BUY INVESTMENT REAL ESTATE?

Since we have talked about the stock market, it is important that we talk about the real estate market, too. Both of these markets contain a big chunk of your unknown future. As of this writing, this is what I know and want *you* to know about real estate.

It was not a normal trend in 1999 when technology stocks and the overall stock market were going up by 25 to 80 percent a year. This kind of overvaluing is now also occurring in some areas of the country in real estate. This overvaluing of real estate is not normal either. For instance, the first few years of the new millennium, home prices in many areas of the United States went up cumulatively by 27 percent. In my opinion it's just not normal when home prices rise that quickly. And when something's not normal, eventually a correction occurs. By "correction," I don't necessarily mean that prices go down, but they may just stop/game up. So if you live in a part of the country where real estate is hyperinflated, I would advise you to be very careful about investing in real estate.

I'm not talking about buying a primary residence for you and your family to live in, I'm talking about if you are thinking of buying investment real estate. You must be very careful to know all that you need to know before you take the plunge. Tell yourself the truth, look at what you have, do what's right for you—and *always* invest *first* in the known.

BEFORE YOU INVEST, KNOW YOUR TENDENCIES

Back in 1998 and 1999, the stock market was starting to go up steeply. After watching this for a couple of years, just when the market hit its high, you probably decided, "I can't stand not being in this market anymore," and decided to participate with everything you already had in the stock market—and possibly more. Like Sam in Law 2, you may have even taken some equity out of your home and used it to invest. Then the stock market started to go down, and kept going. And when it came close to hitting its lows in October 2002, what were you probably tempted to do? Sell out, just when it was pretty much at its bottom for that year.

Why did you want to sell out then? For many people the answer was so they could go back into real estate, for that was where people were making money at that time. But in 2004 real estate may be, in some areas, topped out for now. So, please be careful if you're thinking about investing in this area.

I want to teach you when to act and how to know when it is best not to. So here's a quick lesson on what I think you should consider about the future of real estate prices and why I would be very cautious about investing in investment real estate in certain areas of the country. If you are a sophisticated real estate investor, you most likely will always be okay, but if you don't have sufficient working capital and are dependent on a tenant to pay rent so you can pay your mortgage, please think twice before making this sort of investment.

SUMMING UP: THE KNOWN FUTURE

What happens in the stock market, in the real estate market, or, for that matter, in the job market—all of which is beyond your control—is just a little bit of what can go wrong in your own personal financial life. That's why you have to plan for unforeseen events and protect yourself.

I cannot end this chapter without saying that, in order to prepare for both the known and the unknown, you really should have a will and or living revocable trust, a durable power of attorney for health care, a power of attorney for your finances, and the right kind of long-term care insurance (if you can afford it). If you're young and have dependents, please get the right amount of term life insurance and health insurance; unless you do, you really are not dealing with the common calamities and unforeseens that can affect you and your family. (For more information on the workings of all those necessities of life, see my other books and my website.) Please take action and get yourself these things.

KNOWING AT ALL TIMES WHAT IS BEST FOR YOU

What I really want you to understand is that you *can* prepare for the unknown future in ways that will protect you. Do you want to hold the possibility of not knowing what to do when something happens or do you want to hold the probability that everything will be as good as it possibly can be if the unknown were to happen? If Law 4 can help you to make the right, safe, and wise decision—and it can—then I will be happy.

I want you to know how to apply every law in this book to your life, for you are the most important asset that you have. When you are powerful in regards to your money—by doing that which you know you should do, by doing that which you know makes you safe, by doing that which takes the unknowns out of your life—*then* you are putting all the laws of money into action. Through taking the actions described in this chapter, you will protect yourself, your loved ones, and your money.

Now that you know how to become powerful over your money, the next and final law will show you how to become powerful in and of yourself. The next law is: Always remember: money has no power of its own.

Law Number 5

MONEY HAS NO
POWER OF ITS OWN

When I first started writing about money and talking about it on television, my mother was horrified. I wrote about my mom and dad, and the hard times we experienced financially when I was growing up. I wrote about the many times I messed up with money myself as I was finding my way as an adult. My mom would say, "Suze, I have spent my whole life hiding the truth from everyone and now you go on TV and tell the whole world we didn't have money? How can you do that?"

In time, however, she stopped being upset with me, and even came to approve of what I was doing. People who ran into her would thank her for letting me tell the truth about our situation, because it had been their situation too, and their neighbors' and friends' situation. Few people talk openly about their finances or tell one another the same things they say behind closed doors. My mom learned that telling the truth about money can be liberating.

Today my mom is eighty-nine. She and I now spend more time talking about the years that she may or may not have left than we talk about money. Just a few months ago, I asked her during one of these conversations, "What is the most surprising thing that you have learned in your life?" Her answer shocked me. She said that finally, after all these years, she had come to realize that she was more powerful than her money. When I asked her what she meant by that, this is what she said.

SUZE'S MOM'S LESSON

TRUE POWER DOES NOT RESIDE IN A BANK ACCOUNT

Suze, even though it is getting harder for me to live alone, at this point I can still cook for myself and for you and your brothers, I can drive myself to the grocery store to get what I need whenever I need it. And that, my dear Suze, is more than almost all my friends can do at this point in their lives—regardless of how much money they have. When your father died, I thought my biggest problem was going to be that I didn't have enough money to be okay for the rest of my life. Remember? That was before you had any money. Because I thought I didn't have enough money, I felt powerless. I'd inherited this condo and a small sum of money, but even so I had no idea what to do with them. Little by little, though, with your help, I learned how to make ends meet and work with what I had so that I could create what I now have today. So, today, I *do* have enough. In fact, I have *more* than enough. But the money, to my surprise, is not what is making me feel powerful. Don't get me wrong . . . Thank goodness I have it. It gives me great peace of mind to know that I can pay my bills, go to visit my sister in Florida, and go out to eat whenever I want.

However, all the money in the world would not be enough to enable me to do all that I do at my age on my own. I look at my friends, the few who are still alive, and now my greatest fear is that one day I will end up in a nursing home like many of them and not have the power to take care of myself. Money is not the solution to that problem for me, and that surprises me.

My mom is right.

Money is definitely a vital force in your life, but as my mom was saying, it is not your life force. Where many people tend to go wrong is that they somehow think, just as my mom did years ago, that money will make them powerful. I can't tell you the number of times I've been talking to someone who is in serious financial trouble and all of a sudden she looks up to the heavens and says, "God, I wish I had some more money." Money is never a permanent solution to any problem. Money can come in to your life but it can also go out. Look at all the people who have won millions in the lotteries—many of them have less today than they did even before they won.

You already know that wishing or praying for more money will not solve your problems, or you wouldn't be reading this book. Nonetheless, I want you to redefine money for yourself. Many people define their own self-worth by how much money they have. But it's *you* who give your money its energy, force, and direction. *You* give it potential, meaning, and life. When you do, your actions with money enable you to keep what you have and create what you deserve in your life.

I know this truth can be difficult to accept, because the world we live in does seem to define everything according to monetary standards. But this law was really brought home to me in another way.

SUZE'S LESSON

A PENNY LOST IS A LESSON LEARNED

One hot summer day in New York City, I was taking my favorite walk along Third Avenue, past all the wonderful stores with their window displays offering everything under the sun—fancy furniture in one store and simple trinkets in the next. Summer is my favorite time of the year in New York, and I took this same walk every day, crossing Third Avenue at Fifty-ninth Street and continuing up the avenue past Bloomingdale's. I had turned this walk into a daily ritual, one that I loved.

An integral part of my ritual was bending down in the middle of Fifty-ninth and Third to try to retrieve two pennies that were embedded deep in the tar in the middle of that well-trafficked intersection. Both these pennies had been there for as long as I could remember. I usually used my bare hands to try to pry those pennies out (no tools allowed in my game), and more than once I drew smiles or puzzled looks from others crossing the street. My efforts were tied to the timing of the lights, and my little game ended each day when I had to stop to let the traffic move on. This had become quite an obsession with me. I remained convinced that one day I would set free at least one of those pennies.

On this particular day—the hottest I can remember in New York City, so hot in fact that steam was rising from the sidewalks—I was passing my penny pit, as I called it. I bent down, dug in a nail, and pulled on one of the pennies. The tar was very soft, softer than it had ever been, and it seemed to me that the penny moved—for the first time ever. I continued digging and pulling on this one penny, ignoring the fact that I was utterly destroying my thirteen-dollar manicure. I could feel the penny moving, the tar yielding. With one more tug, to my amazement, it came up. I have to tell you, I felt as if I had just won the lottery. I was jubilant. I had set that penny free. I tried for a second to get the other one out, but the light was changing, the traffic was threatening, and I decided to let the other penny alone. I was as happy as I could be with my accomplishment.

And then this is what happened. While I was waiting at the next corner for the traffic light to change again, I started to flip this penny, throwing it in the air and having just a great time with it. I was already thinking, "What will I do with this penny that I've been trying to get for years, now that I finally have it?" At that moment, I accidentally dropped the penny. I watched as the penny—moving as if in slow motion—landed on its side, rolled a few inches, and went right down into a drainage grate. *Gone!* I could not believe it. It was like a bad joke. It had taken me years to get that penny, and just a few minutes to lose it.

MONEY HAS NO POWER OF ITS OWN

This little adventure with a penny was a graphic lesson for me and a new way of looking at money. With my own eyes, I saw how money—or in this case, a penny—was unable to do anything on its own. The penny had been totally inert and would have stayed right where it was, forever and a day (just like the other penny, which is *still* there) until some other nut took a serious amount of time to pry it out of that tar and spend it, save it, or lose it, as I did.

What happens to that penny, or any penny, depends completely on a person's actions. Do you see that money has no power of its own? All its power flows through you.

PEOPLE FIRST, THEN MONEY

As a group, the first four laws create a road map to help you take control of your money both financially and emotionally. Law 5 focuses even more on your inner power than Law 3 (Do what is right for you *before* you do what is right for your money). It's one thing to know what is right for you and your money and another to have the power to act on that knowledge.

So to personalize this law for you, please ask yourself these questions. If you have been taking actions with your money, and you still don't feel powerful in your life, why don't you? And if you have been using money as a substitute for power, why is that?

Remember Lee, from Law 2, who really did not understand at the time how powerful she was? About two years after she told me that story, I ran into her again and had the chance to catch up on what had been happening with her.

LEE'S LESSON, PART TWO

Money Is Not a Measurement of Personal Power

Walter and I have now been married quite a few years, and, well, things seem to be getting a little rougher. I'm not sure why. Now, we spend time fighting over trivial things, like what to have for dinner and why he won't agree to let me move the furniture around. He also seems not to respect my work, although that's not so trivial, is it? I think he'd prefer that I quit so I can do things with him when he wants to go out. I don't want to quit. I like my work and making money, and I certainly can't imagine being totally financially dependent on Walter.

I think that, because Walter has purchased everything in our apartment with his own money, he thinks he has power over all these things—even me. I think he may believe deep down the only reason someone would love him is because he has money. I don't think he has a clue about why I really do love him. I think he feels strong and powerful because of what he has—his money. Who would he be without his money?

A few years ago, I really thought that if I didn't have Walter in my life, I'd go back into debt or not be able to make it on my own. Now, I see that's not true. I know who I am with and without money, and I wish I could show Walter a way to measure himself and me with a different standard than money.

What is really going on for Walter? In my opinion, he is confusing having more money with having more personal power, as so many people do. Walter may need to learn one of life's greatest lessons, that the earthly source of his own power and the power behind his money both start and end with him.

I hope it's clear that people who have money don't always have power, and people without money sometimes do.

MORE QUESTIONS TO ASK YOURSELF

I want you to ask yourself the following questions, circling yes or no.

Do you believe that . . .

* If you had more money than you do right now, would you actually have more personal power than you currently have? Yes / No
* If you had less money than you do right now, would that make you personally less powerful than you currently are? Yes / No
* Do you think that, because your spouse or life partner makes more money than you, he or she has more power in your relationship? Yes / No

How did you answer those three simple questions? The only true answer in my opinion to all of them is no.

DEFINING POWER

The thesaurus says that power is authority, control, influence. Of course you have control over where you spend your money, but you have to exercise that control. You also have the authority as well as the influence to decide how much money you need in your life. Having more or less money does not give you personally more or less power.

So if you answered yes to any of the above questions, I ask you to make sure you do the exercises in the Guide to Law 5 in the back, where I will ask you to do this particular exercise again before taking on the others. It is essential that you really believe that money has no power of its own, that you really understand and feel that you are *the one* behind the earthly power of your money, that you always have been and always will be. You bring the power or lack of power to each situation and in every one of your relationships.

THE LAWS OF MONEY AND RELATIONSHIPS

The truth is, in most cases *you* can live in accordance with these laws on your own. But anyone you choose to let into your personal life must also choose to live by them. When you start to follow the laws in this book, you will find that being surrounded by others who don't understand or follow these laws will one day start to affect your money and your life—and you most likely will find yourself in financial trouble, even though you haven't done a single thing wrong. For instance, a needy friend asks for yet another loan and you feel so guilty you give it to him from money that you have been saving to pay your property taxes; but he does not pay you back in time and now you are the one in financial trouble. Another example: your spouse is overspending on your joint credit card and refuses to cut back. Over this and other issues, you divorce—and your ex-spouse claims bankruptcy and now you are responsible for his credit card debt.

DON'T BE AN ACCOMPLICE TO A
FINANCIAL LAWBREAKER

As caring a person as you may be, you must *not* help others to break these laws of money—no matter what kind of relationships you choose to enter into. Just as you wouldn't hide stolen goods for a crook in the street, you cannot be an accomplice to the financial lawbreakers in your life. This is not easy to avoid, but you must not do it. You must put Laws 1, 3, and 5 into effect in all your relationships—tell the truth, do what is right for you, and remember that you are the one with the power, not your money. So don't do things for others that render *you* powerless. It doesn't help you and, in the long run, it won't really help them either.

What should you do if people in your life are breaking the laws of money? Talk with them. Try to get them to see why they are making these mistakes or doing things with their lives and their money that are hurting them—and might be hurting you and others too. But *how* you talk to people about money is important, because discussing personal finances, especially when they aren't exactly perfect, is one of the most difficult conversations to have. Keep in mind that, although you now know different, *most* people do equate their self-worth with their money. They want the world, and especially people close to them, to think that they are doing just fine financially. So, you may find it easier and more constructive to have these conversations if you start out by talking about your own attitudes and emotions about money, rather than about the dollars and cents that are actually at stake. To give you some other examples and guidelines on how to do this, please see the Law 5 section of the guidebook.

THE EBB AND FLOW OF MONEY

Whether you are in a relationship or currently on your own, one thing is inevitable and that is the ebb and flow of money. It's like the ocean. It goes in and it goes out. If you always remember that money has no power of its own, and that your worth is not defined by your money, then when you have less, you won't suddenly start thinking, "Oh, I'm no good. I'm a failure. I have less money. I'm worthless." No, it's just your money—it's not you.

And if you have more money, you won't think you're greater than others. You won't begin to look down on your friends and family, or show off your wealth. No, you will know how to spend your money wisely, how to offer it in charity, share it, and take care of it. You can be positive when you have less money, and you can be appropriate when you have more.

INNER STRENGTH

This fifth law is different from the others. This law is a mental attitude you must have. It puts forth not some external action you must take, but a way to think about yourself and your life, no matter what happens. You have to remember not to judge yourself by the money you have. And you have to remember that you will never gain personal power through money.

I put this law last because sometimes, no matter what you do right in life, things can still go wrong. Even if you've been practicing the four laws and they've been working for you and protecting you, something unforeseen could happen. With this fifth law as your financial roof and shelter, and with the support of the other four laws, you won't freak out and say, "I don't know what to do. I'm paralyzed and powerless in the face of this problem." No, you will know *you* still have the power to act, and to follow the laws to start creating all that you deserve all over again.

HAVING POWER OVER YOUR MONEY

Having power over money means that you recognize that *money is your servant.* It's here to *serve* your purposes as well as the world's purposes. Having power over money really means you have power over your life. You determine what you need and want, and then use your money to obtain it or to create that which you feel you deserve.

The bottom line is: power over your money is not being enslaved by your need for it. Of course, you need to eat, you need to have shelter, you want education. But who you are and what you want to create, as I have stated many times, and as the laws state and imply, all starts with you and you alone.

LAW 1

Only you can decide to stop lying about your money—maybe you have been spending more than you earn, or pretending to others that you have more than you do. Only you can decide always to tell the truth.

LAW 2

Only you can decide to let go of your financial past, look at what you have today, and take actions based on your current situation.

LAW 3

Only you can know what is right for you and take action on that and then do what is right for your money.

LAW 4

Only you can decide how to invest your money, how to take actions to secure your life and make sure that you and your loved ones will be fine in the long run because of what you have done with your money. You do this by first investing in the knowns of your life.

LAW 5

Only you have what it takes to make your life personally powerful, to make your money grow. And your power is unique to you.

I hope you will choose to act on all these laws of money. This fifth law really encompasses the other four. Those four will definitely help you come fully into your own power, understand better than before who you are, and engage with Law 5. As you make these laws part of your everyday life, you will naturally come to see how much power you do have and how much you can create.

GOD, I LOVE MY LIFE

Here we are at the end of Law 5 as well as the end of all these laws of money. I hope that you now believe that money runs through all your relationships with other people, and it runs through their relationships with you. And it is your power over who you are and over your money that will determine the ways in which money flows into and out of your life, and how that flow makes you feel about others and how it makes them feel about you.

It may never be your desire to have much more money than you could ever possibly need, but your power over your money and these laws is what will seal your financial fate. Please remember that these laws are just a roadmap, tool kit, and lifeboat for your own personal financial journey. But in the end it all comes back to you and your relationship with yourself and your relationship with your money.

In the pages that follow, I have provided a guidebook that helps you put these laws to work in your own life situation. Please use it. Fill in your particular information and answers to the questions, and review and reinforce every one of the laws again by doing the exercises provided. This will help you weave these laws into the fabric of your thinking, your actions, and your life.

I so want you to understand that the intention and the goal of these five laws is to help you create a personal foundation to stand upon that will support you all your life. The result, of course, is solely up to you because it is you who really must take action. But the actions that you take according to these laws will hopefully always allow you to keep what you have and create what you deserve. Which brings us to this last question for this law: What is it in life that you deserve for all your efforts? Let me tell you what I think.

SELF-EFFORT AND GRACE

If you do all that you can do to create all that you can have, then this is what you deserve:

⁕   You deserve to love and respect yourself.
⁕   You deserve for others to love and respect you.
⁕   You deserve to be loved for who you are.
⁕   You deserve to know that you don't have to agree with everybody in this life, and everybody doesn't have to agree with you, but that does not mean you are right or they are wrong.
⁕   You deserve to have that which keeps you financially safe and sound.
⁕   You deserve to have a home you can call your own.
⁕   You deserve to not to have to worry about ending up on the streets powerless and penniless.
⁕   You deserve to know your own thoughts.

And—

⁕   You deserve to be who you are.

The only way all this will come to you is through your own effort—made under your own power—and made possible through grace as well.

Throughout this book and particularly in this law, I talk about power. But this is the only law in which I have added the word "earthly" before the word power. Why? I do it because I want to be very clear that I personally do believe in an ultimate power that watches over us, protects us, guides us, and wants the absolute best for us. Sometimes, however, we just don't take the power that has been given to us to make those heavenly wishes manifest here on Earth in our own lives—which brings me back to where the book began: the parable of the man in the hurricane who did not take the help or the power that was sent his way. The help is always there. You just need to grab it.

To bring this law, as well as this book, to a close, I'd like to tell you about the greatest life lesson I have ever learned. I hope that in some way it will becomes yours as well.

SUZE'S GREATEST LESSON

TAKING FINANCIAL FLIGHT

A few years ago I came to understand that when we all enter this world we do so with two wings. One wing is the wing of grace, and whether you know it or not, that wing is flapping by your side, supporting you, twenty-four hours a day, 365 days a year, from now through eternity. The other wing, which you have to consciously activate, is the wing of self-effort. This wing has got to flap equally hard as the wing of grace. When it does, you will have flight, flight into the world of unlimited possibilities, where anything and everything is possible for you. Then and only then will you understand how truly powerful you are, and that you have all that it takes within you to keep what you have and to create what you deserve.

I ask you, please, learn these laws, and abide by them, so that the lessons of your life will be bountiful, and so, at the end, when you look back over all that you have been through, you can say, "God, I loved my life." I wish this for you from the bottom of my heart.

The Lessons from Law 5: Money Has No Power of Its Own

✦ You give life and power to your money.

✦ All money flows through you—you are the source.

✦ You have to recognize that you are powerful, no matter how much or how little money you have.

✦ You must choose to have only people in your life who live by the laws of money. If you choose to have people who break the laws of money, that choice will eventually become a lesson of life.

✦ You are the one who brings the power or lack of power to each situation and in every one of your relationships.

✦ Always remember, the most important thing in life when it comes to your money is people first, then money, then things.

EPILOGUE

———◆———

*E*very once in a while I am asked in an interview if I have any regrets. Would I change anything in my life? In my typical Suze way, I always snap back and say very passionately, *"No.* I love my life, and I would not have changed one thing." But then, when I am sitting by myself or just thinking about all that has taken place in my life, becoming a *New York Times* best-selling author, writing and coproducing public television specials, having my own TV show, being a contributor to *O The Oprah Magazine,* traveling around the world to speak to people about money, I realize the answer I give to those interviewers is not true. I do wish I could change one thing, but I know that I can't, so maybe that is why I answer as I do.

The last time I saw my father was a few weeks before he died, in 1981. He was in the hospital and I had been a stockbroker for about one year at that time. He was so proud I worked for Merrill Lynch that he had even opened up a small account there, just so I would have a client at first. On that last day, right before I left his bedside, he looked at me and asked, "Suze, who is going to take care of you and your mother?" I said, "Don't worry, Pop, we will be just fine. You gave us everything we could ever need or want." When I said those words, I did not really believe that we would be just fine, but at that moment I did not care, for I said those words in the hopes that they would comfort my dad. But I do not think that those few words did the trick, for I could tell by the empty look in his eyes that he had wished he had done a better job financially speaking and that he could have left a legacy of wealth to take care of those he loved.

What a shame to die with thoughts of sorrow for what you wished you had done, instead of with incredible joy for what you did do. But my regret is that my father never got to see that everything is more than fine for my mom and me. He never got to see how his stories, his suffering, his mistakes, his persever-ance, his greatness in never giving up, no matter what, helped to teach me the laws of money that helped make me the success that I am today. I want him to know. I wish he could see me now—I wish it so badly I cannot tell you. I wish it not only for me, not only for my mom, but also for him—so he could just know how great he really was. He is the personification of a greatness that cannot be judged on the size of a checkbook but one that can be judged on the size of his contribution to life. I miss you, Papa, and, just so you know, we *are* more than just fine and for that and all the lessons of life—I thank you.

THE
LAWS *of*
MONEY
GUIDEBOOK

GUIDEBOOK INTRODUCTION:

PUTTING THE LAWS TO WORK IN YOUR OWN LIFE

By now, you've read through all the laws of money and read the stories of some people who were challenged by their life situations but who helped themselves by working with the laws. Perhaps you've thought about the lessons they learned and tried to relate them to lessons you've learned in your own life. Let me ask you a question:

Right now, without looking, can you name all five laws?

Sometimes, we get so engrossed in the details of a situation and embroiled in all the dramas that we and others go through that we forget the basic reasons the situation or drama occurred. Even though I explained why I was telling the stories I chose to illustrate the laws in the preceding chapters, *this* guidebook is designed for you to work with your own story. The exercises in this guidebook will help you step back from the details of your own life drama to look hard at the bare bones and causes of any financial trouble in which you are involved, so you can bring it to a satisfactory close, be more, and have more.

For the five laws of money to help you, they need to be able to rise up in your mind whenever you need them. One easy way to make them do this is to single out the most important word of each law for you. You want to isolate that word and remember it so that you can apply it instantly when you need it in your life.

YOUR EXERCISE

I'm going to list each of the laws fully. Read it once, then immediately, without thinking about it, circle the *one word* that stands out for you in the law. These are going to become your personal power words. Ready?

> Truth Creates Money, Lies Destroy it
> Look at What You Have, Not at What You Had
> Do What Is Right for You *Before* You Do What Is Right for Your Money
> Invest in the Known *Before* the Unknown
> Money Has No Power of Its Own

Write in the spaces provided below the one word that you circled above:

_____

_____

_____

_____

_____

Here's what I came up with:

Truth

Have

Right

Known

Power

Keeping the Laws with You at All Times

How close was your list to mine? Probably pretty close. Even if it wasn't, you can use your list, or take mine, to do the next step. I want you to make these laws portable and easy for you to hold on to, and a single word—or five of them that you personally have responded to and remembered—is a good way to do this. Basically, you've just made the five laws into your personal power laws.

Next, I want you to take your word that you circled and make a question out of it. As an example to follow, here are my words in question form:

What is the **truth**?

What do I **have**?

What is **right** for me?

What is **known**?

What is **power**?

Please write your words in the form of a question below:

What _____

What _____

What _____

What _____

What _____

USE THE LAWS IN YOUR LIFE

After you have taken your key words and put them into the form of your own personalized questions, I want you to commit these five words to memory. Five to nine items have been shown in psychological studies to be the easiest number for most people to remember. You remember many complicated numbers and items every day—your best friend's or your partner's phone number, your different ATM and computer passwords, what to put in your children's backpacks, your family's schedule—so this won't be a chore.

Whenever you start to get confused about what you should do with your money or even whether you should buy something, I want you to think of your personalized laws in the form of questions that you can ask yourself at any time.

Look at the word "confused." Confused. Do you see how the three letters "**use**" are part of the word "conf**use**d"? I want you to understand that the best way to keep yourself from being confused in your financial life is to *use* these laws every day. Keep these laws at your financial fingertips to get a grip on any financial situation in which you are not exactly sure what you want to do.

From now on, I want you to take those personal power questions with you in your mind's eye. Start to notice how you can apply them in everyday situations. For instance, when you are in the midst of a conversation or a decision and you find yourself feeling uncomfortable, worried, unhappy, or stuck because you don't know what to do, think about your personal power laws and see if you can ask them of yourself and apply them to this particular situation. You will find that they will help you discover the answer that you need. This process will help you enforce your own financial law-abiding behavior and will also help you find a way out of the current dilemma. Your own personal code of law will also help prevent you from getting into difficult financial situations.

EXAMPLE

You are in a situation (such as Patrick was) in which some old friends call and want you to come on vacation with them. They tell you it will be great fun and cost you only a few thousand dollars. They say you cannot say no, that *all* your old friends are figuring out a way to come, and so can you.

You want to go, you don't want to say no, you don't want to show others that you are not doing as well as they are financially. But you know you shouldn't go. Ask the five personal power questions to yourself.

Now, write down the current financial situation about which you are confused or worried. To help you phrase your own questions, I've included sample questions related to Patrick's situation as a guide.

Your situation:

_____

_____

Example:

Should I go on vacation with my friends or not?

Now pull out your five power questions and answer each one as it applies to your dilemma. For instance, you might write:

What is the truth?	*I want to go, but I cannot afford it.*
What do I have?	*I have no debt and I love that.*
What is right for me?	*Not spending money I do not have.*
What is known?	*If I go, I will have debt that I might not be able to pay off if I lose my job.*
What is power?	*The ability to tell my friends and myself what my true situation is and that I have to do what is right for me.*

When you see it very clearly like this, you see the laws at work and you make the right decision for you.

Try it in another situation that's worrying you. Maybe it's a family or work situation. The questions get easier to pose to yourself and answer each time you do it.

As you practice these questions over and over again, you will see how these laws naturally become a part of your financial soul. They are your own financial rules of the road and will help you get you to where you want to go. Any time your financial engine stalls, you can take out your tool kit of your personal power laws and questions to help repair yourself and keep you plugged into your power.

WHERE DO YOU WANT TO GO?

Before I give you more ways to use all five laws in your life, I want you to ask yourself where you want them to take you.

In the spaces below, write out a few financial goals that you would like to accomplish in your life within the next six months, the next year, the next two years, or as far into the future as you would like to think right now. Just for the heck of it, why not throw in one goal that you might think is totally out of reach but that we will call your dream goal.

By giving form to your dreams in this written list, you are one step closer to bringing them about. Write them down and make them happen. Tell yourself the truth about what you want and what's right for you. When you do, you will see how you can put the five laws of money and your own power to the task.

Your Financial Goals

Next Six Months

_____

_____

_____

_____

_____

_____

Next Year

_____

_____

_____

_____

Next Two Years

_____

_____

_____

_____

Your Dream Goal

_____

_____

_____

_____

MAKE A DATE WITH YOURSELF

Go to the calendar where you keep important dates that you *must* remember and write in the dates that correspond with the time periods above. If today is June 5 and you have a six-month goal of improving your FICO score (page 266) by 20 points, I want you to write that goal in on December 5: ("FICO score up 20 points") During the six months until that date, you will use the laws of money and your own effort (your power) to improve your financial practices and your FICO score. On that date, you will check to see if in fact your score has increased. For long-range dates of a year or more, you'll obviously need a long-range calendar.

Remember, when you make a date with yourself, you should always want to keep it. When you do, you are putting *all* five laws into effect.

GETTING IN YOUR FINANCIAL LIFEBOAT

So now that you know where you want to go, and you have your key words and questions to serve as your engine to help you get there, you still have to make sure that your financial lifeboat is seaworthy. Maybe you can see storm clouds gathering in your life or maybe you are already in the middle of your own financial hurricane.

No matter what your situation, now or in the future, you can be sure that the laws of money will help you if you use them. The laws don't pertain only to people who have a lot of money. They don't pertain only to people who *don't* have a lot of money. The laws of money apply to every person who has any money at all in his or her life—and as I see it, that's absolutely everyone.

Therefore, this guidebook is designed for you to use, no matter what your financial situation, to help you take what you have read earlier in *The Laws of Money* and put it to work for you and your money. I believe that as you do the exercises throughout this guidebook, you will see with increasing clarity how the laws can help you take powerful actions in your life and with your money.

Please do *all* the exercises in every section. There are no shortcuts to making sure you have mastered the lessons. The more you invest in this process, the more you and those you love will be able to keep what you have and create what you deserve.

Now, let's put Law 1 to use in your own life.

GUIDE TO LIVING LAW 1:

TRUTH CREATES MONEY, LIES DESTROY IT

In its own way, the first law lays the basis for all the other laws in this book. Everything we say, think, and do really gets its footing in the world from this essential law—financially and in every other sense.

I believe that you and your money are one. You earn it, you spend it, you invest it. Your money all starts with you, even within you, as we learned in Law 5. So, as I was creating these laws over the past few years, I wanted to make sure that each was based in an action that you could take. Each action had to hold true in any and every situation that you could come up against in your life as a whole, not just in your financial life. Even the fifth law, which is different from the others, requires a *mental* action.

Behind every really powerful person, however, is one very simple, vital practice. That practice is telling the truth. If a financial foundation is built on lies, it will eventually crumble, no matter how powerful the person or institution may seem. If you really want to create what you deserve in this lifetime, you must create it in such a way that you yourself are proud of all the actions you take. You and your money have to become one with the truth. Speak the truth, think the truth, and take actions that are based in the truth. It is simple to say and to think that you will, but it can actually be difficult to do, as you've no doubt discovered already in your life. And it's difficult not because you are a bad person or you set out one day with the intention of lying. It is just easier sometimes not to tell the truth or the whole truth, isn't it?

FIRST IMPRESSIONS

Let's face it. In a consumer-oriented society such as ours, it's easy to fall into the trap of using things—clothes, shoes, the house we buy that we cannot really afford, cars, boats, furniture, jewelry, cell phones, and even computers—to make an impression on others. In a way, when you buy those things on credit cards it is not because you need them but because you want to impress others—or yourself—with what you *have* rather than who you *are*, and when you do, you are living a lie. Maybe it's just a little blue-light-special kind of lie, but it is a lie, nonetheless.

I expect you might read that last statement and think, "Gosh, Suze, that is really harsh. It's not like I'm stealing. I'm putting the items on my credit card and I intend to pay them off, so why do you call that lying?" I call it lying because the reasoning that gives rise to your action is not truthful, even though your action itself is not technically a lie. You tell yourself that you have to have that item—that's Lie 1. You may want it very badly, but chances are you do not *have* to have it. You tell yourself that you can afford it—that's Lie 2. If you have to put it on a credit card that you cannot pay off in full at the end of the month, you cannot afford it. You may *want* to be able to afford it, but at this point the truth is you cannot.

You promised yourself at the time you purchased it that when the bill came in you would pay it off in full. But when the bill arrives, the credit card company requests only $10 instead of the total cost of $300, and you think, "Well, that's a bargain," so that is all you pay. That is Lie 3. You pay only the minimum because you really do not have enough to pay the other bills that *are* important and you are afraid to let go of your money. Three strikes, you're out.

Over the past twenty-odd years, I have seen too many so-called little white lies cause people to end up in bankruptcy court. All of these serious financial problems started with just one seemingly harmless purchase or a tiny financial fib. Let's call it what it is from now on. It really is a lie. Using the word "lie" does sound harsh, but a look at the dictionary may provide some guidance.

DEFINITION OF A LIE

Merriam-Webster's Collegiate Dictionary gives the following definitions:

> When "lie" is used as a verb, the definition is "to create a false or misleading impression."
> When lie is used as a noun, it is "something that misleads or deceives."

I want you to be very honest with yourself right now. Let's say you have found this incredible watch that costs a few thousand dollars. You know that you cannot afford to buy it, but you do anyway so that others will think you are doing really great financially. Isn't it true that when you charge something like that on a credit card for those reasons and you know that you cannot afford it, in some way you are doing this to create a false or misleading impression, since you cannot afford to be wearing that watch or article of clothing or piece of jewelry? So you have actually done something that misleads or deceives everyone who sees you with that watch.

I use this example because when I was at the height of my own lying to others and to myself, back in 1987–1988, I went

out and charged a Cartier panther watch just so the person I was
with at the time would be impressed. *Webster's* would say I was
lying. I would say so, too, now.

YOUR EXERCISE: HOW DO YOU USE YOUR MONEY?

To make sure you're telling the truth and creating money as well
as you can, let's find out how you use your money. Do you in
fact use your money and the possessions it buys to speak the
truth about yourself, or do you use them to make false impressions? To sharpen your focus on the ways that you communicate
about yourself every day, read the following statements, then
rate how true each one is of you by marking "Always,"
"Often," "Sometimes," or "Never."

	ALWAYS	OFTEN	SOMETIMES	NEVER
1. To feel good, I need to dress like the people I'm with.				
2. I think I won't get ahead at work unless I look the part, or better than the people I work with.				
3. I'm embarrassed to admit it when I can't afford to do what my friends or colleagues are doing.				

	ALWAYS	OFTEN	SOMETIMES	NEVER
4. If I were going to a tenth class reunion, I'd go into credit card debt just to look fabulous, even if I couldn't afford it.				
5. I'm afraid people will think less of me if they find out that I am in debt up to my eyeballs.				
6. I believe that friends will like me better if I pick up the tab in a restaurant, even if I don't really have the money to do it.				
7. Leasing a loaded SUV that makes me look prosperous matters more to me than buying a car I can afford.				
8. I'm determined to give my kids the best of everything, no matter what it costs.				

	ALWAYS	OFTEN	SOMETIMES	NEVER
9. When the conversation turns to stocks/ investments or income, I'm likely to make it sound as if I have more (or less) or make more (or less) than I actually have or do.				
10. If a friend asked me for a loan, I would do it even if I didn't feel comfortable about it.				

Look at how often your checkmarks fall into the columns above. Look especially at how many fall into the "Always" column. Then rate yourself below.

- If you checked "Always" **8–10** times, your need to impress others has a high potential of leading you to choices that will destroy your financial life. Be on the lookout for the white lies in your life. You most likely have credit card debt and could be on the verge of serious financial trouble.
- If you checked "Always" **5–7** times, you're playing with the truth about your finances. You'll pay a high price for making so many decisions based on what others think of you, rather than on what is honestly best for you. You probably leased a car instead of buying one.

✦ If you checked "Always" **2–4** times, you are vulnerable to the desire to impress others. Be alert to urges to falsify your situation. You are prone to exaggeration in words more than in actions.

✦ If you checked "Always" **0 or 1** time, you tend to be true to yourself in the company of others. Keep up the good work. No credit card debt here!

WHAT ARE YOU AFRAID OF?

When it comes to money, just about everybody has chosen, is choosing, or will choose lies over the truth many times in a lifetime. Sometimes we know we're doing it, sometimes we don't. In fact, a lot of the time, we tune out our own lies. Why? Because they are serving some purpose in our lives. We get something out of them, even though they don't serve our best interests in the long run. The truth of our situation makes us frightened of the future, makes us feel bad about ourselves, or makes us doubt the interest and affection of others. The lies we tell ourselves and others temporarily relieve some negative feelings, but they always come back to haunt us and even harm us sooner rather than later.

YOUR EXERCISE

I want you to take a closer look to see if in fact you tell financial lies and, if you do, to see whether you can find out what you get out of them. When one tells a financial lie, it generally is very subtle, and usually is what I call a "self-lie." Whenever you tell yourself something so that you feel better about yourself, that is a self-lie. And really those are the most dangerous of lies.

You may still be thinking, "No way, I do not tell lies about my money at all." If you actually think you have no room for improvement in this area of your financial life (and I hope you are right), I still want you to do the exercise below to make sure. And I want you to pay particular attention to question 9. So, let's find out:

Read the following phrases, then finish them as completely and honestly as you can. I've given you some examples that are in italics, just to help get you thinking.

1. I'm usually tempted to buy something that is too expensive for my budget when . . .

   (I want to impress others with how great I look. Or I just want my outfits to make me look great, so I justify the cost.)

   _____

   _____

2. I don't open my bills when I get them, and I usually do not total up how much I really owe, because . . .

   (I know I do not have the money to pay them and it scares me to death to face that reality.)

   _____

   _____

3. Even though I know when my bills are due, I find that I ignore paying my bills on time because . . .

   (I am afraid to let go of the money I do have, so I try to hold on to it for as long as possible, just to make me feel better.)

   _____

   _____

4. I have not told anybody that I have credit card debt because . . .

   (I am afraid that they will think that I am a loser.)

   _____

   _____

5. When I exaggerate about what I have, I do this because I want others to . . .

   (Think that I'm more of a success at my job than I think I actually am.)

   _____

   _____

6. I know I should be putting money away for my retirement, but I don't because . . .

   (It will mean that I can't do/get what I want right now.)

   _____

   _____

7. I know I need to make changes in my situation, since I am pushing it in every financial way possible, but I don't make those changes because . . .

   (At this point it almost seems hopeless, and it is easier just to keep paying the minimums on my credit card than to take all the energy and time to fix it.)

   _____

   _____

8. I know when I am lying to others and I do it because deep
down inside . . .

*(I'm afraid that they'd stop liking me if they knew the truth
about me.)*

_____

_____

9. I know when others are lying to me, but I just let it slide
because . . .

*(I just don't want to fight with them and it just seems easier
to let it go.)*

_____

_____

Look back over the sentences you have completed. How many
of the sentences did you find to which you could relate? Were
there any that you could not complete? If you were able to relate
easily to all the questions and even had answers similar to the
ones I provided, I just want to say it's good that you now see
how and where you've been lying to yourself. You are not alone
and you are certainly no different from most people in the
United States. We somehow have developed the habit of pushing
away money and the responsibilities that come with having it as
if money were an enemy. Isn't it odd that we treat money as an
enemy, yet we always want more of it?

These answers at least give you a starting point. At least now
you are not lying to yourself *about* lying to yourself. The path of
the truth has to start somewhere and, believe it or not, it just

started with this exercise. Eventually, I want you to get to the point where you can look at those questions and be able to say truthfully, "No, I do not do any of those things, so I cannot answer those questions." Becoming free from this self-deception *is* possible for you. I know it's possible, because those self-lies are how I used to deceive myself. *I* also used to feel all those emotions that those lies give rise to years ago, when I was a serious financial liar. Today, I look at those questions and can answer all of them truthfully. I simply do not do any of those behaviors anymore. And I no longer have the fear, worry, or insecurities that went with them. When I stopped lying, I made that U-turn and I have never looked back again.

You can do it, too.

In case you are the rare person who cannot relate to any of the questions and behaviors above, you have already begun walking the path of truth. For that, I congratulate you. Now, please think about those you know and make sure that the answer you gave for question 9 was truthful. Further, please think about your friends who do lie. As we have seen in Law 5, in discussing money and relationships, having friends or family who lie about money will most likely hurt you in some way at some time. You do not help others when you allow their financial lies to continue. So if you have friends who lie—and you know of their deceptions— you might want to share this book with them and tell them how you're going through the process of financial truth telling.

In my own life, once I started to see how I was lying, I also was able to catch myself as a lie was forming. Sometimes I would let the lie go through but I began to be able to identify when they were coming up and why I was motivated to tell a lie or to tell the truth. Let's take what you've just done and push it a little deeper.

THE SOURCE OF THE PROBLEM

All right. You now know whether you have to work more on telling financial truths. If you are on the path of lies, you hopefully want to make a U-turn. The key to making that U-turn is understanding how you got to where you are now. You can be sure that along the way, you came upon numerous crossroads, and at some of those crossroads, you chose a lie instead of the truth. I want you to try to retrace your steps.

I want you to take however much time is needed to remember each of the crossroads in detail. In the spaces provided below, I want you to state the facts of the choice you made, what happened as a result, what other choices would have been possible, and what might have happened had you chosen differently. Then answer the questions that follow.

I've given you room to note four different crossroads. If you need more, use a separate piece of paper and reproduce the format you see here. Be sure to tuck the extra page or pages into your guidebook so you can refer to them later.

YOUR EXERCISE

State what your biggest financial problem is right now:

Next, use the crossroads chart to trace your steps back to how you got to where you are now.

For example, let's assume Patrick from Law 1 is doing this exercise.

What is your biggest financial problem?

"The fact that I have no money to pay my creditors who keep

calling."

His first crossroads might look like this:

Crossroads #1

What is the earliest choice you made that you can now see led to where you are?

THE CHOICE YOU MADE	WHAT HAPPENED	THE CHOICE YOU COULD HAVE MADE	WHAT COULD HAVE HAPPENED
When my friend called to invite me on a vacation, I did not have the courage to say that I could not afford it.	I ended up with $33,000 of debt on my credit card, no job, a house that needs repair, and a dead car battery that I had to fix.	I could have just told my friends that I did not then have the money to go, because I had a good chance of being laid off.	I would have been home to return the call to my old employer who wanted to hire me. I would have been there to protect my house against the storm.

Your turn—see what happens when you do this exercise.

Crossroads #1

What is the earliest choice you made that you can now see led to where you are?

THE CHOICE YOU MADE	WHAT HAPPENED	THE CHOICE YOU COULD HAVE MADE	WHAT COULD HAVE HAPPENED

What was the truth about you and your finances at this crossroads?

_____

_____

If you lied, what lie(s) did you tell yourself or others to cover up?

_____

_____

Why did you think you needed to lie in this situation? What did you hope to gain or protect yourself from losing by your lie?

_____

_____

What was the actual result of the lie?

_____

_____

Crossroads #2

What is the earliest choice you made that you can now see led to where you are?

THE CHOICE YOU MADE	WHAT HAPPENED	THE CHOICE YOU COULD HAVE MADE	WHAT COULD HAVE HAPPENED

What was the truth about you and your finances at this crossroads?

_____

_____

If you lied, what lie(s) did you tell yourself or others to cover up?

_____

_____

Why did you think you needed to lie in this situation? What did you hope to gain or protect yourself from losing by your lie?

_____

_____

What was the actual result of the lie?

_____

_____

Crossroads #3

What is the earliest choice you made that you can now see led to where you are?

THE CHOICE YOU MADE	WHAT HAPPENED	THE CHOICE YOU COULD HAVE MADE	WHAT COULD HAVE HAPPENED

What was the truth about you and your finances at this crossroads?

_____

_____

If you lied, what lie(s) did you tell yourself or others to cover up?

_____

_____

Why did you think you needed to lie in this situation? What did you hope to gain or protect yourself from losing by your lie?

_____

_____

What was the actual result of the lie?

_____

_____

Crossroads #4

What is the earliest choice you made that you can now see led to where you are?

THE CHOICE YOU MADE	WHAT HAPPENED	THE CHOICE YOU COULD HAVE MADE	WHAT COULD HAVE HAPPENED

What was the truth about you and your finances at this cross-roads?

_____

_____

If you lied, what lie(s) did you tell yourself or others to cover up?

_____

_____

Why did you think you needed to lie in this situation? What did you hope to gain or protect yourself from losing by your lie?

_____

_____

What was the actual result of the lie?

_____

_____

WHODUNIT?

Now look back over the events and choices that put you in the situations you now want to change. Were other people involved in any of your crossroads decisions? They might have been family members, advisors, friends, or people with whom you work. Whoever they were, list them below. Beside each name, record the part you believe the person played in your decisions. Be honest about how you felt at the time. Did you feel that they coaxed you to do something you didn't want to do? Were you afraid of how they would react, depending on what you chose? Were you trying to impress them or fit in with them? Did you want to be like them or participate in what they were doing? Search your memory for what you thought and felt and write it down as honestly and thoroughly as you can.

On the first line, Patrick's answer is given as an example:

THE PERSON   HIS OR HER ROLE

Friend who called   Enticed me to go on a trip
_____   _____

_____   _____

_____   _____

_____   _____

_____   _____

Based on what you now know, who was ultimately responsible for the choices you made? Was it the people you've listed, or was it you?

_____

If you answered anybody but you, you are still lying to yourself.

I can now admit that no one forced me to tell the financial lies I told. I was totally responsible for choosing to spend money I didn't have so that I would still appear to be "successful." It was not until I admitted the lies to myself that I could start living the truth.

ACTING FROM A PLACE OF TRUTH

This is an important moment of truth for you. You've studied Law 1: "Truth Creates Money, Lies Destroy It" in the text as well as here in the guidebook. You've looked in some detail at some of your own financial lies and the results that they led to. Now it's time to make the U-turn to change your direction. I want you to identify every person or situation that you must address to stop the financial lies.

- Do you need to ask someone to pay you back a loan that is seriously overdue?
- Do you need to call the collection agencies that have been calling you (and whom you have been telling, "No one by that name lives here"), and work out a payment plan?
- Do you need to tell your wife that you bounced $12,000 worth of checks and you do not know what to do?
- Do you need to tell your friends that you have $8,000 of credit card debt?
- Do you need to tell your kids that you may not be able to afford to pay for their college education?
- Do you need to tell your boyfriend that you do not want to continue to eat out at those fancy restaurants every night, because you cannot afford it?
- Do you need to tell your sister that you are not lending her the $5,000 she asked for?

If any of these situations are true for you, *yes*, you do need to act to correct them and bring out the truth of your financial life. You *need* to act just as you should always have the need

—and feel the need—to tell the truth. Just as you need air to breathe and food and water to live, you need truth to be your constant companion in your financial life or you will not get to where you want to go.

Use the grid below so that you can see for yourself what you need to do to practice telling the truth and acting on the truth, so that you can create money in your life.

My U-*turn* Calendar

ACTION DATE	WHOM/WHAT DO YOU NEED TO ADDRESS?	WHAT ACTION CAN YOU TAKE RIGHT NOW?	WHAT OUTCOME DO YOU HOPE FOR?

Take a moment to look over what you have just written down. Then use the column at the far left to give yourself a specific time to take action. Act on at least one of the items *this week*. Continue to choose at least one item for action every week until you've checked off every item on the list.

Now you're ready to move on to Law 2: "Look at What You Have, Not at What You Had." Keep in mind, even as you move ahead, that you need to keep practicing Law 1 and telling the truth again and again, every day. It will help you form the foundation of an empowered future.

GUIDE TO LIVING LAW 2:

LOOK AT WHAT YOU HAVE, NOT AT WHAT YOU HAD

Memory is a wonderful part of what makes you human. And your memories can serve you well, giving you a sense of where you come from, keeping past experiences available to teach you in the present and future, and offering a sense of how far you've come in your years of life. However, when you try to hang on to the past or paralyze yourself with regret for past mistakes, memory can also dig you into a big hole.

Law 2 is all about making *today* your starting point. And I don't mean just this once. In fact, *every* new day is just that, a new starting point from which you can build the future that is right for you. You may have had negative financial experiences in the past, which convinced you that you don't have power over your life and your money today. Or you may have just suffered financial losses that make the past hard to let go. In either case, you need to bring yourself up-to-date with what you have, or you will be stuck in a place that steals your energy and your power. You can't make wise decisions and take appropriate actions based on information that is outdated. You also have to figure out who *you* are today, because no doubt you have changed in some ways, just as your finances have.

This section of the guidebook is designed to help you put the past behind you and get a firm grip on the present. As you work through this section, remember to keep practicing Law 1: be as honest as you can be. Exercise the truthfulness that you have been honing in Law 1. Give yourself as much time as possible to think carefully through the concepts and lessons of this law and to complete each exercise. Just as you are learning to stay on the path of truth, you need to use that truth to deal honestly and consistently with what you have *right now*. This practice is crucial to seeing your dreams come true.

SHOULD'VE, COULD'VE, WOULD'VE . . .

Remember when you could mail a letter for fifteen cents? Or go to a movie for a dollar or two? Even if you're not old enough to remember those days, you certainly have seen the effects of inflation every year of your life. You wouldn't expect to be able to mail a letter for the postage cost of five years ago. Nor would you expect the ticket taker to let you into the latest movie at an outdated rate.

In the following exercise, you will have the opportunity to give the past a last, long look. But instead of dwelling on it, wishing for it, or regretting it, you will be examining it as a souvenir, something that helps you remember but that you can then set dispassionately on a shelf or even throw away. You will look at it, understand it, and then leave it behind.

In this exercise, I give you a series of phrases to work with. Read each one, then use the space provided to finish the thought in your own words with reflections on your past. You may want to use extra paper to go through this process more than once, and think through a number of different circumstances from your past. As you go, keep in mind that this little stroll down memory lane is all about catching up with the reality of right now.

Remember Lee's story? Even after she had married Walter and was doing fine, she was haunted by a time in her life when her finances were a mess. Because she could not let go of that past, she continued to believe that she was the kind of person who needed to be "rescued" by someone else—in her case, by her new husband. It took her a while to see that *she* is the one who works hard for the money she earns. *She* is the one who saves and is building a strong financial foundation for herself. But her past experience had become an accuser that told her that, because she used to have less, she *is* less. She worked through that and now sees the difference. In a similar way, I want you to work through any past experiences that are holding you back from seeing what you have clearly and from moving forward to create what you deserve.

YOUR EXERCISE

In the space provided below, I want you to write about a past financial mistake that you made or past action or feeling related to money that you can't let go of.

1. When I think about my financial past, the *one* thing that keeps coming back to haunt me is . . .

PATRICK—*Because I did not tell my friend the* **truth** *when he*

called that I could not afford to go on that vacation, my life is a

financial **wreck***.*

SAM—*I* **lost** *almost* **everything** *I had because I refused to sell Cisco*

when it was still at 80. I cannot believe that I bought it to begin with.

MAYA'S MOM—*I hid our financial* **trouble** *from my daughter, Maya,*

and didn't tell her the truth when she was younger; now she blames her-

self even though she had nothing to do with it.

2. This part of my past stays with me because . . .

*PATRICK—I am still having to pay **today** for all that I did back then. I still don't have a job, I still have almost $30,000 of credit card **debt**—and I still have not told my friends the truth.*

*SAM—It's hard for me to forget, because everywhere I go there is news about the stock market, Cisco, Intel—all those high-flying technology stocks—and when I come home every day I drive right by the **house** I loved so much and had to sell.*

*MAYA'S MOM—I will never be able to **give** my daughter her graduation day back. I ruined it for her, so every day when we talk and I hear the **pain** in her voice and she asks me how my money is doing, it reminds me of what happened.*

_____

_____

3. As I look back at this time and circumstance, it makes me feel about myself that . . .

*PATRICK—I am a real loser—that I **sold myself** down the river when I took that rafting trip.*

*SAM—I am **scared** to **death** ever to make a move with money again.*

_____

_____

*MAYA'S MOM—If anyone knew the **truth** about me, they would just*

*be totally **disgusted** and in fact they would be right.*

_____

_____

Review your answers. Please look carefully at the negative feelings or ideas you have brought into the present from this past event or circumstance. To emphasize this for yourself, I want you to pick out two words that jump out at you and circle them. Please write those words below in the order of the questions.

Patrick circled the following:

1. Truth and Wreck
2. Today and Debt
3. Sold and Myself

Sam circled the following:

1. Lost and Everything
2. House and Loved
3. Scared and Death

Maya's Mom circled the following:

1. Trouble and Maya
2. Give and Pain
3. Truth and Disgusted

Please write the two words you circled in your answers to each question:

1. _____

2. _____

3. _____

Those six words, in that exact order, will most likely contain the story of what you are holding on to. I want you to create a story out of the six words that you circled. Let me show you what I mean using our three examples.

Patrick's Words

1. Truth and Wreck
2. Today and Debt
3. Sold and Myself

String those words together in the exact order of the questions: truth, wreck, today, debt, sold, myself.

Now let's see how Patrick might use those words to show himself how he feels using those exact words:

Well, the **truth** is I am a **wreck today** because of the **debt** I created when I **sold myself** short for not sticking up for what I knew was right.

Sam's Words

1. Lost and Everything
2. House and Loved
3. Scared and Death

Lost, everything, house, loved, scared, death.

I **lost everything**—my **house** that I **loved** living in, my money, my girlfriend—and now I am **scared** to **death.**

Maya's Mom

1. Trouble and Maya
2. Give and Pain
3. Truth and Disgusted

Maya, trouble, give, pain, truth, disgusted.

My heart will never heal because of the **trouble** that I caused my daughter, **Maya**, today. When I think of what I did **give** her, all I can answer is **pain**. The **truth** is, I'm just **disgusted** when I think of myself.

_____   _____   _____   _____   _____   _____

Please write your six words above in a row. Now create a story using these words about the situation that you are having a hard time letting go.

_____

_____

As you look at your story and you think of your life today, I want you to ask yourself some more questions:

Can you turn back the hands of time?
Will you ever do what you did to create the situation that
    you are in again?
Can you no longer afford to buy food?
Are you living on the street because you no longer can
    afford a roof over your head?
Have your kids or friends decided that they are never talk-
    ing to you again because of the actions that you took?

Would you ever repeat that mistake again that led to the feeling that you are still holding on to?

Did you learn the life lesson that you were supposed to learn from this situation?

Do you get it?

I am sure you answered no to every one of those questions except the last one, to which I hope you answered yes. If you've learned from this experience, you must accept the fact that that is what you are here for and what you need to take and work with. You have to move forward.

REARVIEW MIRROR DRIVING NOT ALLOWED

Now we're going to take those same words from which you created a story of defeat and write a story of what you *do* have today. You're not going to write about what you had, or about what you could have had, but about what you do have. With the aid of Law 2, "Look at What You Have, Not at What You Had," use the words that led to your financial problem to see what you do have and what you can create. Think about the life lesson that you learned when this happened to you and try to express it in your own words. Let's first see how Patrick, Sam, and Maya's Mom have done with this exercise.

Patrick

Truth, wreck, today, debt, sold, myself.

The **truth** is that I really am no longer a financial **wreck**. As of **today**, I am straight with all my creditors. Even though I still owe them money, little by little, I am starting to pay off that **debt**. I have not **sold** my car, I now have a newly repaired roof over my head, and in the end I have learned a good lesson about **myself.**

Sam

Lost, everything, house, loved, scared, death.

So what if I **lost** most of my money back then? I am currently still making a great living and am saving little by little to rebuild **everything** that I want to have. I can save and get another **house** sooner rather than later. And all that really matters is that today I am **loved** by my friends and family, and I've even got over being disgusted with myself. I now know that I have what it takes to go through the worst of times and there really is nothing in life I am **scared to death** of at this point. I'm putting my past to rest and appreciating what I have.

Maya's Mom

Maya, trouble, give, pain, truth, disgusted.

Well at least I know that **Maya** is not in financial **trouble** today herself. My husband and I give ourselves a little credit— we know that the **pain** is not as bad today because at least our daughter knows the **truth** and still loves us. I can be proud now and no longer need to be **disgusted** about what I did, especially since I am taking actions today to set it straight.

Now, it is your turn:

Take those six words and tell your story with them, of what you do have today that you are proud of. You can make it as long as you need, use your words over and over again if you want, but only use them in a positive sense. If you see that you are using them negatively, stop, and restate that fact in a positive truth that reflects what you have today, not what you had or lost months or years ago.

————— ————— ————— ————— ————— —————

Now, write what you feel the life lesson is that you have learned. Again, focus on the positive aspects of what you do have today.

_____

_____

You may have a number of situations or memories that you did not include. If so, repeat the entire exercise—all the questions, starting on page 214, and the exercises that follow them—on a separate piece of paper. If you do this for every piece of your past that you are hanging on to, you'll discover resources you didn't know you have. You'll be amazed at the new sense of freedom and power you feel as you truly let go of the past.

———

THREE GATEKEEPERS

Are you ready to let go of what you had? Do you see how pointless it is that you are spending energy and time in hanging onto the past? To help keep you in the present let's meet three guardians, or gatekeepers, who can guide you.

It can be very hard at times to live in observance with Law 2. That's because it can seem as if it is easier to live in the past than to create the present that you want to have. When I was betrayed by my assistant and had the problem with the paperwork that I told you about in the first chapter, I can remember saying to myself, "Suze, if you can only look at everything that has happened as a present that you're willing to unwrap, you would see what's really there. You would see what you have and not what you had lost." Well, in the long run, I finally did that, but I have to tell you it took years for me to get there, because even after I started to tell the truth about my money, I wanted to blame my assistant, I wanted to feel like I was a victim, I wanted somehow to hold on to what was no longer true. I needed to take stock of what was true in every area of my life.

And then one day I was at a lecture and the speaker said something that changed my life and helped me to stay focused on what I did have and not what I had. I would like to share that teaching here in the hope that it will help make it easier for you always to look at what you have rather than what you had.

From this day forward, in order to keep yourself grounded in the truth of who you are, who you want to be, and what you want to have, everything that you say, think, and do has got to pass through these three following gatekeepers, which are questions that you ask:

Is it kind?

Is it necessary?

Is it true?

For instance, every time you find that you are saying to yourself or someone else, "I was so blind/irresponsible/unlucky," *stop*. Check your thinking and your words. And ask yourself these three questions. Is it kind to you? Is it necessary to say or hear? Is it true about you *today*? If your answer to any question is no, you don't want to let your words or your thoughts pass all three gatekeepers. This means that you are to pause and realize that you are stuck in ways of thinking and acting that will not allow you to keep what you have and create what you deserve. Think of these gatekeepers as the doors through which you have to pass to move from what you had and who you were to what you have and who you are. Any thought or attitude that cannot pass the gatekeepers is destructive to your financial future and in direct violation of Law 2.

TAKING STOCK OF WHAT YOU DO HAVE

If you've been honest and thorough so far, you're doing a terrific job of letting go of the excess emotional baggage of the past. Now it's time to come to terms with the present condition of your money as well. One of the questions I am asked most, no matter what the conditions of the market or the economy happens to be, is: What should I do with the stock or mutual funds that I currently own? Should I sell them? Should I just hold? Many people become paralyzed when they feel the need to do something with their money or investments. Today, you may also worry about whether you can trust any financial expert to give you the right advice so that you can make the right move.

Let's just play investment advisor for a bit. I have always said that if you want to find the best financial advisor, just look in the mirror. No one will ever care about your money more than you. Do not allow yourself to become paralyzed and do nothing at all because you are mired in the memory of what something used to be worth. Doing nothing sometimes is one of the most damaging actions you can take, if your money is already in the stock market or other volatile investments. Here is an exercise that will help start the process of taking action *today*.

YOUR EXERCISE

The chart opposite focuses on your investment portfolio. You need an accurate, up-to-date picture of what you own and how it looks in light of your current financial situation. This chart will help you pull the information together and give you an opportunity to assess realistically where you stand, as well as what you think you should do with your money/investments. So, take a deep breath, gather together your most recent statements from any and all investment accounts, and follow the six numbered steps, which follow the chart.

Know Whether You Want to Keep/Sell or Hold

1 NAME OF STOCK/ MUTUAL FUND/ OTHER INVESTMENT	2 DATE OF PURCHASE	3 TOTAL PRICE PAID	4 CURRENT TOTAL VALUE	5 GAIN OR LOSS	6 WOULD YOU BUY IT NOW?

Complete each step:

1. In column 1: List every single stock, mutual fund, piece of real estate or other investment you own, including variable annuities, variable life insurance, and whole life insurance.
2. In column 2: Write down the date when you purchased this investment.
3. In column 3: Fill in the total price that you paid, including all commissions. For example, if you bought 1,000 shares of Cisco at $30 per share and you paid $47 in commissions, write $30,047 here.
4. In column 4: Fill in the total value of what that investment is worth today. Again, if it were Cisco and it was worth $16 today, you would write in $16,000.
5. In column 5: Write the gain or loss that you currently have in each investment. You get this figure by subtracting the total price you paid in column 3 from the total value in column 4. For instance, if you paid $30,047 for Cisco and it is now worth $16,000, you currently have a loss of $14,047. At least you see where you really stand now with this investment today.
6. In column 6: For every investment that you currently own, ask yourself, If you did not own this today and you had this exact amount of money that you have in column 4 in cash, would you—this very moment—buy this stock, mutual fund, or other investment? Answer yes or no in the final column.

If You Answered Yes

The investments you would definitely buy if you could again today are obviously ones that you feel comfortable with. Now to check out how realistic your feeling is, look at column 5. If you have a gain and you still feel comfortable, just make sure that all is still going great with that company. If so, that gain should hold. If you have a loss, however, make sure you understand how that investment is doing and what will happen to turn it around. This is a nice and easy place for you to get in touch with what you have today in terms of your investments.

If You Answered No

Any investment to which you gave a no above is one that you now need seriously to consider selling, or at least to find out more about the reason for its disappointing performance. If you would not buy that investment again today, that means you do not really think it will go back up. So why are you holding on to it? Most likely, because you are waiting and hoping and praying—just as Sam did—that it will at least return to the value at which you purchased it. But in reality, that stock may never come back to that original value or even close to it. You have to face your fear of taking your losses or that fear will keep you from any gains. Take a good look now at the numbers in column 5 above and please understand that, whether they are on paper or not, those losses or gains are what you have today. Whatever you *had* no longer matters.

Next, copy the names of these investments in the second column of the chart below.

After you have gone through each individual investment, place a checkmark in the first column beside that stock, mutual fund, or other investment, and record the action you've chosen in the last column provided, with the date you implemented it.

✓	NAME OF INVESTMENT	ACTION TAKEN/DATE

What you see before you in this chart is a record of your clear-sighted, proactive fresh start. You have looked realistically at the questionable investments you have, and you have made a thoughtful response. You should repeat this process of review and action at intervals throughout the life of your investments. Things change: your circumstances and time of life; the health of the businesses in which you are invested; the national or world economy. All of these can turn a good investment into an undesirable one. As the person in control of your money and your life, you can't afford to do less than stay up-to-date with every investment you have.

THE REST OF THE PICTURE

You've taken a close look at one aspect of your financial picture. There is more to it, of course, and I want you to get in touch with that before you have finished this guidebook. You need to keep your financial situation in clear view for scores of decisions every week of your life. You can do that only by knowing what money you have, how much money you owe, how much money flows in every month, and how much flows out.

In Law 4 of the guidebook, you'll make a detailed examination of all of these pieces of your financial life. For now, I just want you to believe me when I tell you that you do not need to feel frightened or discouraged by the difference between what you had in the past and what you have now. Whatever your situation was or is, you should be gaining a sense of power over your money, because you are gaining knowledge about yourself and your real situation right now. From knowledge you build strength, and from strength you can take action that will move you forward in a positive, life-building direction.

The work you have just done in this guidebook will help you ground yourself in the present. I hope it also helps you know more about yourself and what you are made of because in Law 3, you'll be focusing on how to do what is right for you before you do what is right for your money. Keep going!

GUIDE TO LIVING LAW 3:

DO WHAT IS RIGHT FOR YOU *BEFORE* YOU DO WHAT IS RIGHT FOR YOUR MONEY

When you focus on money in your life, it's easy to forget what money is all about. You start thinking about how much money you "need," where you should put your money, and what your money goals actually are. These are important questions to answer, but they are not the *first* questions you need to ask. Especially in today's world, it's easy to buy the idea that the more money you have, the more you as a person are worth—which logically means that having more money is always better than having less. It's a short hop from such thinking to wanting at least the *appearance* of having a lot of money, no matter what your reality is or what it may costs you spiritually and psychologically.

Put on the brakes right now, because you need to have one thing completely clear in your mind before you go any further. In your relationship with money, *you* are the living being and money is your tool. Money does not define you or make you more valuable as a human being. It cannot love you, keep you company on a dark winter evening, or listen to your life stories. If you have any confusion about this, go back right now and reread the text section on Law 3, starting on page 47. As you make your life decisions—about relationships, career paths, possessions, or whatever—think of money as the protector of your goals and dreams or the servant to them. That's all it is, because as you learned in Law 5, money has no power of its own. If you want do what is right for your money—if you want to put your money to the absolute best use *for you*—you have to know yourself. You need to understand who and what is most important to you. You also have to find and maintain a clear vision of what you want your life to add up to.

This section of the guidebook is designed to help you find or regain that clear vision. Only you know the answers to the deepest personal questions about you. In the following exercises, you'll have an opportunity to explore and answer those questions and discover what your answers mean in relation to your money.

Take your time here, and be completely honest with yourself. It is the "heart" of the matter, and getting it straight will help the rest of the laws work for you too.

WHAT'S AT THE TOP OF YOUR LIST?

Knowing who and what matters most to you is key to dealing with money. So I want you to take a quick inventory right now of your priorities. Do this by taking a quick glance at the words below and circling the 10 that are the most important to you in your life:

home	freedom
God	cultural events
health	my education
my children	creative opportunities
my parents	volunteering
adventure	new experiences
physical fitness	romance
security	charity
friends	spiritual reflection

travel

time off from work

education funds for my kids

my significant other

a vacation home

control over my own life

gourmet food

myself

community service

great clothes

entertaining at home

career

active fun

the arts

lack of worry

church

my animals

money

my car

my siblings

jewelry

my looks

After you have circled the ten words, use the spaces below to list them in the order of what is the single *most important* down to the tenth most important:

1. _____

2. _____

3. _____

4. _____

5. _____

6. _____

7. _____

8. _____

9. _____

10. _____

Take another look at what you have written. Does it really represent who and what matters more to you than anything else? If not, make the needed changes now. Understand that what you've listed is right *for now*. It might change at another time of your life, it might not. But for today, this should really represent your priorities.

ONE IMPORTANT QUESTION

Before you move on, here's one more question. Did you put *you* on the list? If not, why not? There was the word "myself" in the middle of all those words—that word meant you—did you add it to the list? You probably put other people on that list, but I bet you did not put yourself. If you did, where did you put yourself? Are you anywhere near number one on your own top ten list? Or did you think, "It would be selfish of me to put 'myself' on that list?"

Do you see how easy it is to dismiss your own importance in your own life? And in a section on the law that you put yourself first? Honestly, who is the one who is most responsible for your welfare? You. And who will suffer most if you neglect to care for yourself, physically, emotionally, or financially? That's right. You.

THE BIG QUESTIONS

The more you remind yourself of your top priorities (and by now I hope that you added yourself to that list, in the top position), the more likely you are to make life and money decisions that reflect those priorities—that is, to do what is right for you. But there's more to doing what is right for you than focusing on who and what matters most to you. You not only have priorities. You also have a temperament, an emotional makeup, and a unique style and background. So let's put your "top ten" into the context of *who you are*.

Read each of the questions below, then use the spaces provided to answer truthfully, clearly, and fully.

What makes you feel secure when it comes to your money? (For example: Is it a big sum in a safe account? Knowing that you have enough available if something bad happened? Holding only blue chip stocks in your portfolio? Keeping $500 in cash in a sock under your mattress?)

_____

_____

_____

What makes you happy when it comes to your money and your friends? (Having enough to give gifts to those you love? Traveling to exotic places? Treating your friends to dinner?)

_____

_____

_____

What makes you afraid with regard to your money? (Losing your current job? Losing your home? Losing the value of money that is in your 401[k] plan?)

_____

_____

_____

The exercises above only touch on who you are when it comes to your money. But they can begin to give you an idea of the sorts of things that need to be in your life to make you happy, give you a sense of security, and build a life that is good for you. Remember the story of Chris and Amy? Same financial situation—completely different responses. What I want you to get a feel for here is the kind of responses *you* have to many different parts of your life. Money flows through all of your life aspects, and you will not know what is best for your money until you know what is best for you.

FINDING YOUR UNIQUE BALANCE

As you know by now, decisions regarding what is best for you don't depend entirely on hard and fast rules. Because you are unique, your best interests will depend on decisions and preferences that are yours alone. You'll need to find the right balance for you between good money practices and your own sensibilities.

Please read each of the statements in the chart below. They represent a variety of emotions that can help you identify your comfort zone with money. After you've read each description, choose the response that *most closely* describes you, and write the number value in the space provided.

	AGREE COMPLETELY	AGREE SLIGHTLY	DISAGREE SLIGHTLY	DISAGREE COMPLETELY
	4	3	2	1
1. When in doubt, I play it safe.				
2. I need to know that I can't lose any of what I have.				
3. It bugs me not to know what is going to happen next.				
4. I want my friends to tell me how they feel about me.				
5. I always have my car serviced before I take a long road trip.				
6. Tradition is extremely important to me.				
7. I always get my ducks in a row before I do something important.				
8. It's better to keep doing what I know I do well than to experiment with new things.				

9. I dislike games that include an element of gambling.				
10. I prefer buying an item with a fixed price over bidding at an auction.				
11. I get a charge out of suspense in my life.				
12. I prefer to travel to new places on vacation rather than return to the same place year after year.				
13. I expect things to turn out well.				
14. I enjoy the "thrill of the chase" phase of romance.				
15. I'd rather have a job that pays me commissions when I perform well than one with a fixed salary.				
16. If I were offered a seat on the space shuttle, I'd go in a minute!				
17. If I want something, I go for it, even if I can't quite afford it.				

	AGREE COMPLETELY 4	AGREE SLIGHTLY 3	DISAGREE SLIGHTLY 2	DISAGREE COMPLETELY 1
18. I enjoy trying new things, even if it means making mistakes.				
19. When I travel for pleasure, I prefer to "play it by ear" rather than fix an itinerary.				
20. I don't bother with a regular schedule of doctor's checkups. I go when I'm sick.				

Scoring

Category A: Add up the scores you gave yourself on questions 1

through 10. Record the total here: _____ .

Category B: Add up the scores you gave yourself on questions

11 through 20. Record the total here: _____ .

The highest score you can get in either category is 40.

If you scored 30 to 40 in category A, you have a high need
for safety, comfort, and known quantities in your life. And you
should take that into consideration when you are making investments.

If you scored 20 to 29 in category A, you tend to pay it safe
but don't mind taking a chance some of the time.

If you scored 30 to 40 in category B, you have a high interest in adventure, risk, and challenge.

If you scored 20 to 29 in category B, you prefer to take
chances if it means greater gains, but you still want some stabil-
ity and predictability in your life.

Chances are, as you look at your scores, you'll realize that
you have a combination of both elements in your makeup. But
if you're like most people, you fall more into one category than
the other; this information about yourself is important to keep
in mind as you make decisions about your money. The quality of
your life can be affected just as much by how you *feel* about
your decisions as it can by the decisions themselves.

Now let's look specifically at how all this translates into terms
of money and investments.

THE FEAR FACTOR SCALE

You've worked in this section on connecting with who you are and what you care about. You've also had an opportunity to reflect on what you fear—that is, what robs you of your joy and peace. Fear is a renegade among human emotions. Once it takes hold, it can quickly career out of control and leave you miserable and paralyzed. The only way to rein in fear is to face it directly and take rational action.

The Fear Factor Scale teaches you how to rein in your fear about money. The following charts will help you to deal with important decisions about how to handle your money *without* fear. By taking a rational look at what you have or might like to have, and testing it against your emotional and intellectual responses, you can make the decisions that are emotionally right for you. Please understand: this is what you do *after* you have done your other homework. For instance, on page 223 in the Law 2 section of this guidebook, you went over your existing investments to make sure that they are still good investments, according to your own research and the advice of a financial advisor you trust. Now you want to take those good investments and test your emotional and psychological responses to holding or selling.

So let's get started by filling in "Current Investments and Assets" below.

CURRENT INVESTMENTS AND ASSETS

List every single investment that you currently have in the spaces provided. Also list all of your other assets, including other tangibles of value.

					NAME OF INVESTMENT
1	2	3	4	5	
1	2	3	4	5	
1	2	3	4	5	
1	2	3	4	5	
1	2	3	4	5	
1	2	3	4	5	
1	2	3	4	5	
1	2	3	4	5	
1	2	3	4	5	
1	2	3	4	5	
1	2	3	4	5	

After you have listed all your investments and assets (using a separate piece of paper, if you need additional room), ask yourself this question:

On the scale of 1 to 5—with 1 as the most positive and 5 as the least (see below)—how do I feel about each investment I currently own?

Use the following descriptions to decide where on the 1 to 5 scale you belong for each investment or asset. Circle the appropriate number for each in the chart above.

1   Absolutely fine; no problem whatsoever.
2   Fine, but a little bit unsure.
3   Not sure how I feel at all, and it is causing me confusion about what to do.
4   Most of the time, I feel sick about this investment, although once in a while I am okay with it.
5   This investment scares me to death; I can't stand to open the envelope that contains information about it, I wake up at night thinking about it, or I am distracted when watching a movie.

Your response will show you emotionally what you would really like to do with the investment you have.

IF YOU CIRCLED	THE ACTION YOU TAKE FOR THIS INVESTMENT IS:
1	Keep the entire investment.
2	Sell 25 percent of the investment.
3	Sell 50 percent of the investment.
4	Sell 75 percent of the investment.
5	Sell it all.

POTENTIAL INVESTMENTS AND ACQUISITIONS

Now let's try the same exercise with potential investments. Make a short list of investments you could imagine considering, if you had $10,000 to invest.

					NAME OF INVESTMENT
1	2	3	4	5	
1	2	3	4	5	
1	2	3	4	5	
1	2	3	4	5	
1	2	3	4	5	
1	2	3	4	5	
1	2	3	4	5	

Once you've listed as many potential buys as occur to you, ask yourself the following question:

On the scale of 1 to 5—with 1 as the most positive and 5 as the least (see below)—how do I feel about investing the entire $10,000 in each potential investment I have listed?

Use the following descriptions to decide where on the 1 to 5 scale you belong for each investment. Circle the appropriate number for each in the chart above.

1   I feel great and happy to buy it.
2   I have a very slight hesitation, but mainly feel great about it.
3   I am really confused I want to buy this, I do not want to.
4   I have a slight desire to do it, but overall I really feel reluctant.
5   The thought of making this investment scares me to death, even if I am afraid to miss out on a great investment opportunity.

Take a look at what the rating you gave each possible investment means in terms of how that action would make you emotionally feel

IF YOU CIRCLED	YOU WOULD FEEL EMOTIONALLY GOOD IF YOU . . .
1	Could take all $10,000 and make this purchase (this *assumes* it's a good investment and the correct time in the market).
2	Held back 25 percent of the money you were going to invest. Assuming that the purchase is a good investment and it's the correct time marketwise, you would use $7,500 for the purchase and put the remaining $2,500 in a money market fund and just continue to see how this investment makes you feel.
3	Held back 50 percent of the money you were going to invest. Assuming that the purchase is a good investment and it's the correct time marketwise, you would use $5,000 for the purchase. Hold the remaining $5,000 in a money market fund and just continue to see how this investment makes you feel.

IF YOU CIRCLED	YOU WOULD FEEL EMOTIONALLY GOOD IF YOU ...
4	Held back 75 percent of the money you were going to invest. Assuming that the purchase is a good investment and, it's the correct time marketwise, you would use $2,500 for the purchase. Hold the remaining $7,500 in a money market fund and just continue to see how this investment makes you feel.
5	Did nothing at all. You do not feel safe with this investment.

This scale works just as meaningfully—if not as prescriptively, since you can't buy 25 percent of an asset like a home—if you're considering a purchase such as a home, a new car, a boat, or a motor home. The point is, you can't do what is right for you without including yourself in the equation. By all means, get the facts about the investment. But once you know that an investment has the backing of your financial advisor or respected analysts, remember also to pay attention to your own gut reactions.

IF YOU ARE A PARENT OF DEPENDENT CHILDREN

I really have to come back to a crucial point. I know you've read what I have to say about taking care of yourself financially before you take care of your children. If Maya's parents had followed that precept, they would be in a very different place today. Their case may seem extreme, but believe me, it happens all the time. And unless you are living Law 3 day in and day out, some version of it could happen to you.

So I'm going to put the pressure on you for this next exercise. Answer the following questions with absolute honesty (remember Law 1!).

* Have you told the truth to your child(ren) from the beginning about your financial situation?
* Have you prepared your child(ren) to share the responsibility for their education?
* Do they understand that their part will be to get the best grades they can, and to think about schools that your family can afford, while you do your part to provide food, shelter, health maintenance, and love?
* Have you let them know how much you love them and that, together with them, you will find a way to help them achieve the most for their lives, even if it is not in the way their friends do it?

If you answered no to any of these questions, you need to make a date right now to bring your children into the conversation. It's never too late for you to learn to put first things first and to take responsibility for your own share of the challenge. Keep in mind that your kids learn some of their most important lessons about living within their means and making responsible decisions for their present and future by watching you. They'll believe what you *do* a whole lot sooner than what you *say*. Are you teaching them by setting a good example? Forget what you've done in the past, if the answer to this question is no. *Start now!*

This concept will be true as well if you're dealing with partners in a business, aging parents, friends in dire circumstances, or colleagues in a community effort. You must take care of yourself first, or you'll have little or nothing to offer others, and your own quality of life will be eroded or destroyed.

PUT IT TOGETHER

Take some moments to look back over everything you've done on Law 3. Ask yourself this:

What do I need to change *today* to put Law 3 into action? (Do you need to deal differently with your investments? If so, be specific: "I need to reallocate my investments so that I can sleep better at night." Do you need to level with someone about your financial relationship to him or her? If so, name names here: *"I need to make a date with Joe this week and talk to him about which colleges can realistically be on his short list, considering our financial situation."* Whatever in your money life that doesn't "fit" should be included here.)

_____

_____

_____

_____

Now write out an action plan for yourself about how you will begin to make the change you just described. Include names, details, and a time frame. An "action plan" is an action plan only if you know exactly what active steps you are going to take and when you are going to take them. For example: *I will call my investment agent tomorrow morning. I will make the earliest appointment with her that she has available. Before the end of* this *month, I will work with her to create a portfolio that really makes me feel good and safe.*

Write down what you plan to do and when you plan to do it by:

I will _____

_____

_____

_____

The next section focuses on Law 4: "Invest in the Known *Before* the Unknown." This law will take all that you've learned and put it into action in powerful and practical ways with your money.

GUIDE TO LIVING LAW 4:

INVEST IN THE KNOWN
BEFORE THE UNKNOWN

It's easy to get confused about what to do with your money, especially when the stock market and economy are volatile. Many people have lost money in the stock market or have been laid off and don't see any new work coming their way. We all notice when the money we're making isn't worth as much as it used to be and it's harder to make ends meet. You don't know whether to buy or sell investments. You want a new house but you don't know whether this is the time to buy, or even if you can afford it.

This section of the guidebook is a way to sort out the ways in which you need to get your money situation straight right now. It will help you bring order to your finances and develop some systematic strategies for getting on course and staying there. Law 4 in the text is so detailed that I need not repeat much of that information here. I have simply provided charts and information that you need to know about such matters as your FICO score and how to pay off credit card debt, some of which was not covered in great detail in the text itself. Please make sure, when working with this law in particular, that you use the information in the text along with the information in the guidebook so that you really do know what to do.

KNOW YOUR EXPENSES

Your biggest financial challenge is to make sure you have the money you need to pay all your monthly expenses. In the text I put forth a plan for you to do that, but its vital to know how much money you will actually need. The first step is to figure out very carefully just how much those expenses are. I don't want you to guess or estimate, but to work from the real figures over the past year.

Follow these instructions to fill out the "My Monthly Expenses" worksheet:

1. Go through your records and receipts for the last complete calendar year. This includes all checks, all credit card charges, all ATM withdrawals and cash advances. You will have to record *every* expenditure you made in those twelve months—if you no longer recall what it was for, put it under "miscellaneous."
2. Record the amount you spent month by month in each category. If any categories relevant to your spending are missing, add them in the blank spaces at the end of the chart.
3. After you've filled in all the categories for the entire 12 months, add up the total for each category and write it in the next-to-last column ("Year's Total").
4. For each category, divide the "Year's Total" by 12. This will give you the *average* amount you spend each month. Write this figure in the last column.
5. Total all the figures in the "Monthly Average" column. Write the figure you get in the final space labeled "Total Monthly Average Expenses."

Keep in mind that you're doing this exercise to get an *average* amount you spend per month. There will be months when you spend less and months when you spend more. I want you to work from the average figure.

Doing this exercise completely is one of the only ways you can really get a grip on the knowns of your life.

MY MONTHLY EXPENSES

	JAN.	FEB.	MAR.	APR.	MAY	JUNE	JULY	AUG.	SEPT.	OCT.	NOV.	DEC.	YEAR'S TOTAL	MONTHLY AVERAGE
Mortgage/ PMI/rent														
Property taxes/ insurance														
Home maintenance, association or condo fees														
Utilities (gas, electric, oil, water)														
Telephone, cellular phone, cable														

	JAN.	FEB.	MAR.	APR.	MAY	JUNE	JULY	AUG.	SEPT.	OCT.	NOV.	DEC.	YEAR'S TOTAL	MONTHLY AVERAGE
Home systems (alarm, pool, spa, cleaning service)														
Garden, firewood, lawn care														
Food, alcohol, restaurants, home entertaining														
Medical, dental, optometry														
Veterinarian														
Insurance (life, health, auto)														

Auto							
Transportation, parking, tolls							
Clothes, shoes, jewelry							
Dry cleaning, laundry service							
Hair, manicure, facial							
Alimony, child support							
Children's education and childcare							
Job training, education							

	JAN.	FEB.	MAR.	APR.	MAY	JUNE	JULY	AUG.	SEPT.	OCT.	NOV.	DEC.	YEAR'S TOTAL	MONTHLY AVERAGE
Professional fees (legal, accounting, counseling)														
Safe deposit box														
Technology (computer, printer, DSL)														
Payments on credit card balances, loans (other than mortgage)														
Bank, credit union fees														

Postage, shipping							
Entertainment (video rentals, movie tickets, etc.)							
Recreation (sporting events, vacations, hobbies, health clubs)							
Donations							
Gifts							
Lottery							
Cigarettes							
ATM cash withdrawals							

	JAN.	FEB.	MAR.	APR.	MAY	JUNE	JULY	AUG.	SEPT.	OCT.	NOV.	DEC.	YEAR'S TOTAL	MONTHLY AVERAGE
Seasonal expenses: firewood, furnace cleaning, summer camp														
Weekly expenses: lessons, cleaning help, babysitter														
Miscellaneous														
TOTAL AVERAGE MONTHLY EXPENSES														$

KNOW YOUR INCOME

Until you have a clear, accurate picture of your money situation, you will not be able to put Law 4 fully to work for you. You certainly have to know how much of your money on average goes out every month, but you also need to put that information alongside how much on average comes in. The actual difference between those figures, whether it's money left over or growing debt, is critical to developing a complete picture of what else you need to know in your financial future.

In the worksheet below, I want you to record every source of income and the amount. Again, be completely honest. If the income from a particular source varies from time to time, please choose an average figure that you feel fairly certain will continue for at least two more years. Any amount that will not continue for two years should not be included. For example, you shouldn't include a loan someone is almost finished paying back to you, or your remaining paychecks if you're working but about to be laid off or retire. Stick to the money you can actually count on, month after month, for at least two years.

When you have filled in the yearly amount of each source of income, total all the figures and write it in the space provided. Then take that total and divide it by 12; this figure is your average monthly amount of income after taxes.

MY ACTUAL INCOME

Yearly paychecks after taxes and deductions	
Predictable bonuses	
Social Security income	
Disability income	
Bond interest income	
Other interest income	
Dividend income	
Rental income	
Gifts from parents (if regular and reliable)	
Loan repayments (if regular and reliable)	
Pension income	
IRA income	
Alimony and child support	
Miscellaneous	
Yearly Total	$
Average Monthly Income (line above divided by 12)	$

KNOW WHERE YOU STAND

Let's see what the information you've just gathered means. In the worksheet below, write the Average Monthly Income figure in the first row. Write the Average Monthly Expenses figure (page 256) in the second row. Subtract the expenses from the income. Write the resulting figure in the "Difference" row. This figure is the amount of your monthly deficit or excess.

Average Monthly Income	$
Average Monthly Expenses	$
Difference (Monthly Deficit or Excess)	$

You may already have known what you've just put in writing. If so, I'm proud of you! If you're like most Americans, however, you're either pleasantly surprised or (more likely) at least a little shocked. That's okay. Consider it a "thanks, I needed that" moment. You can't invest in the knowns until you know what they are! With the information you've just gathered, you're ready to get busy and start to improve your financial future.

CREATE OR INCREASE YOUR EXCESS

If the difference in the chart you just completed came up as a deficit or a zero, you have just demonstrated why you never seem to get ahead. Understand that you can certainly do something about it. You can earn more income, cut back on some of your expenses, or eliminate some or all of your bills. Even if your income exceeds your expenses, it's in your best interest to know how to increase the difference and to do it.

So I want you to try a little experiment now. I want you to go back over your list of expenses and put a checkmark alongside every item on the list that could be adjusted, if need be. Any of the "luxuries," such as meals out, recreational expenses, entertainment costs, and items such as lottery tickets, can easily be tweaked or even eliminated (as in the case of the lottery tickets). You can stop wasting money—for example, on overdue fines on books and videos or late fees on debt payments—by concentrating on returning items promptly or making payments on time. Numerous services that you could do for yourself but choose to pay others to perform—housecleaning, laundry, manicures, accounting, and even cups of coffee—can be shifted partially or completely back into your hands. Only you know how you are spending the money that you don't have or that you could make better use of.

Now go over the items you have checked and choose ten painless changes you could make to your present spending habits. Write these in the spaces below, and *be specific* (for example, "Wear clothes one more time before taking them to the dry cleaner," or "Reduce the housecleaning service from once a week to once every other week, and do a 'once-over-lightly' myself on the off week.") Don't fill in a dollar amount yet.

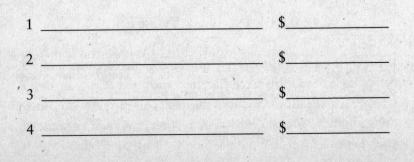

1 _____ $_____

2 _____ $_____

3 _____ $_____

4 _____ $_____

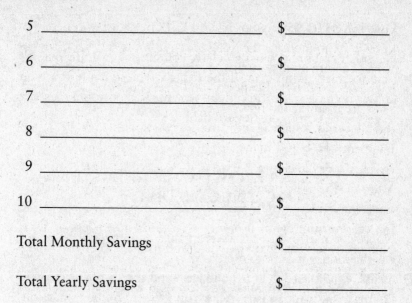

5 _____ $_____

6 _____ $_____

7 _____ $_____

8 _____ $_____

9 _____ $_____

10 _____ $_____

Total Monthly Savings $_____

Total Yearly Savings $_____

Now I want you to commit to following through on each of the savings actions you've just described *for one month*. During that month, carry a small notebook with you at all times. Every time you would ordinarily spend money on one of these items, jot down the amount you *didn't* spend. For example, if you usually get two manicures a month and you choose to do your own manicure, record the amount you saved ($15 × 2 = $30). At the end of the month, add up the total amount of savings for each item. Add those totals to give you the total savings for the month. Multiply that total by 12 to figure out how much you could save in just one year with these few painless changes in your habits.

You'll be amazed to see how it adds up. I hope you'll also see that there are many other ways in which you could change your spending habits to give you more excess income.

FIRST ACTIONS

Now that you know what you have coming in and going out, it's time to start taking care of the expenses in your life that you know you have to get rid of. The very first expense you must act to get rid of is your credit card debt.

USE YOUR EXCESS INCOME TO TACKLE CREDIT CARD DEBT

Nobody can afford to carry credit card debt, even if he or she has the money month to month to keep up with minimum payments. Credit card debt is bondage—and that is not a lesson in life that you want to carry with you. When you buy on credit, you are paying for your present-day desires at the expense of your future needs. That makes you a slave of the past, shelling out current money for things that are losing or have already lost their value. And, because interest on your credit card debt is compounded, you are stealing money from your future income.

What can you do?

First, make sure you have the lowest possible interest rates available on all your credit cards. Then, follow the steps below, and you'll soon be solving this problem.

STEP 1

Figure out what is the absolute *most* you can afford to pay monthly toward your credit card debt. If necessary, refer to the expense and income worksheets on pages 251–258. Write this figure in the space provided.

Largest amount I can put toward credit card debt: $ _____

STEP 2

Use the chart below to write down all credit cards on which you owe a balance. List the card that charges the highest interest rate first, then the card with the next highest rate, and so on. To the right of each credit card account name, record that card's minimum monthly payment. For example, if the minimum payment on your statement is $50, you should write $50 in that column. (Remember, the minimum payment will decrease as you pay down the debt, but I want you to keep paying the minimum you write down—in this case, $50—plus an additional sum I'll talk about in a minute.) In the next column, write the interest rate. In the final column, record the entire balance that you owe on the card.

My Debt

CREDITOR	MINIMUM PAYMENT	INTEREST RATE	BALANCE OWED
TOTAL		N.A.	

Once you've filled in the information on all your cards, add up all the minimum payments and write the total in the space provided. Do the same for all the balances.

STEP 3

Write the figure from step 1 in the space provided below. Write the total of your minimum payments from step 2 below. Then subtract the minimum payment total from the largest amount figure—the result is what you have available to pay down your debt.

Largest amount toward debt   _____

  minus (−)

Minimum payment total   _____

Extra available to pay debt   _____

Let's say, for example, that the largest amount you can apply per month to your credit card debt is $400. Suppose the total that you would have to pay is $275, if you applied the minimum payment to all of your cards. If you subtract $275 from $400, you see that you have $125 extra available.

STEP 4

Instead of treating your extra available money as a bonus check for spending, commit yourself to paying the "Extra to pay debt" amount each month to the credit card with the highest interest rate. Meanwhile, on all the other credit cards, you will continue to pay just the minimum required—nothing more. Continue to do this every month until the first card is completely paid off. When the first card is paid off, do not close the account until you know if it will affect your FICO score—be careful of closing credit cards down (see page 268).

STEP 5

Now repeat the process with the second card. Continue paying the minimum on all the cards. This time, however, take whatever amount you were paying on the first card (now paid off), and pay that *plus* the minimum payment you were paying on the card with the second highest interest rate.

When that card is paid off, begin your payment cycle all over again with each of the remaining cards. In this way, you will keep rolling down your payments until they are all gone.

SET UP AN EMERGENCY FUND

After you have paid off your credit card debt, it is important that you set up an emergency fund as soon as possible. To do so, use the sum you figured out you actively spend each month (from page 256). I have found that most people underestimate what they need by about $500 to $1500 a month. In fact I have no doubt that when you figured out your average monthly expenses, you found that you spend at least $500 to $1500 a month more than you think you do.

I would like you to plan to put aside at least 8 months of your expenses in an emergency fund.

Emergency fund minimum = $ _____ Total monthly expenses (from p. 256) x 8

In the text on page 104, I give instructions on what to do to protect yourself before you have an emergency fund set up.

———

KNOW YOUR FICO SCORE AND WORK TO IMPROVE IT

One of the ways you can help to pay off your debt more quickly is to get the lowest possible interest rates. This depends in part on having as high a FICO score as possible. Your FICO score is simply a value or "grade" given to your credit, based on your past credit performance. In essence, it rates the likelihood that you will repay what you owe. Find out what your FICO score is by logging on to the website www.myfico.com. (This will cost you $12.95.) Record your FICO score here:

FICO Score _____

If your score needs to be improved (in my opinion, it does if your score is less than 720), follow the suggestions below. However, do not be too upset if your score is below the 720 mark—only about 40 percent of the population ranks above 720, but a whopping 30 million Americans have scores under 620. If you are in that large section, or if you are at any level that really makes you want to raise your FICO score, there are several things you can do.

CHECK YOUR CREDIT REPORTS

You ought to review all your credit records at least once a year to make sure that all the information is accurate. Also do so several months before applying for any loan. You can change a mistake on your report—for example, if a payment is mistakenly reported as late—but the correction will take anywhere from one to three months to appear on your report. If you need assistance doing this, please log onto my website, www.suzeorman.com, where I have tools that will help.

PAY YOUR BILLS ON TIME

Paying your bills by when they're due accounts for 35 percent of your FICO score, so this is extremely important for your current payment history. Do everything you can to get your payments in on time, no matter what, especially in the months prior to applying for a loan. A late or missed payment close to the time that you apply for a loan will lower your score far more than an isolated late payment some years in the past. It can seriously hurt your score, sometimes to the tune of about 75 points. That one skipped payment could take you from a good rating to a horrible one.

REDUCE CREDIT CARD DEBT AND DON'T CHARGE AS OFTEN

Reducing your debt figures large in your FICO score. You do yourself a huge favor by eliminating all credit card debt, or at least by not using your cards as often. The goal here is to improve your credit score, and one way of doing that is to widen the gap between what you owe and what your credit limit is. The less you owe, the better your FICO score becomes.

UNDERSTAND THE REPORTING PERIODS

You need to understand how your creditors provide information to credit bureaus. Even if you always pay off your balance at the end of the month, your FICO score may not reflect that. You may actually have a lower score than you deserve and therefore be paying higher interest rates than you have to on large purchases that need financing. On a particular day once a month, your credit card company reports your balance to these agencies. If, on the day before they report, you happen to charge a large sum on your credit card, they will report that you owe that amount of money. Now let's say you pay off that balance at the end of the month. But then, right around the same time of the next month—right before the credit card company reports—you charge a large amount again. As far as FICO can see, you have carried this balance for two months running, which says to them that you are not paying down your card balance. *Ding!* Down goes your FICO score.

BE CAREFUL ABOUT CLOSING ACCOUNTS

Your credit ratio is one of the keys to your FICO score, so it is important that you understand what happens when you close down cards you are not using. Imagine that you have four cards, each with a credit limit of $2,000, for a total combined credit limit of $8,000. In your wisdom, you have only ever used one of those cards, which currently has a balance on it of about $1,500. Your debt-to-credit limit ratio is 19 percent ($1,500 divided by $8,000). If you think, "Well, I am not using my other cards, so I should just close them," be careful. If you close an account you are not using, your FICO score may be affected negatively. In the example, if you have only one card open, which has a credit limit of $2,000, and you have a balance of $1,500, that makes your debt-to-credit-limit ratio 75 percent—bad news for your FICO score. Believe it or not, you just might be better off leaving the extra cards open and unused.

KNOW THAT CREDIT HISTORY IS
IMPORTANT FOR FICO SCORES

Here's another reason that you may not want to close down the credit cards that you do not use. Your FICO score is based in part on your reported credit history. If you have four credit cards that you got more than ten years ago, you have a reported credit history on those cards that goes back ten years. If, however, you decide to get a new card with a better interest rate and closed down all the other accounts, your reported credit history has also been closed down. This will count against you. So sometimes, especially on the older cards on which you do not pay a yearly fee, you may be better off keeping them and not using them. Closing them down and shortening your history may hurt your score.

PAY CASH FOR PURCHASES BEFORE YOU APPLY

The key to getting the best or lowest interest rate when you need a mortgage or to borrow money for a large purchase is to have the highest possible FICO score. Your FICO score goes up when the credit bureaus see your balances going down. Especially in the months before you apply for a loan, be very careful how much money you are putting on your cards. If you need to buy something, buy it in cash if possible. Pay cash when you eat out, go to the movies, shop for groceries, or buy clothes. Hey, if you do not have the money to pay cash for something at this point, just don't buy it! All of these charges could hurt your FICO score.

BEWARE OF BANKRUPTCY

If you declare bankruptcy, you cannot do much to get that score up for a number of years. Bankruptcies stay on your credit report for ten years. Just because you have claimed bankruptcy, however, does not mean that you cannot get credit. In many cases, there are lenders who will be all over you like a cheap suit. They know that, legally, you cannot claim bankruptcy again for at least six years. So during those years, they just love to sock it to you with interest rates that are sky-high. Be careful. A number of people who claim bankruptcy have to claim it twice. Your FICO score aside, in my opinion, bankruptcy is a very serious action to take; you need to seek the best advice and think about it carefully. It may or may not make sense for you in your particular situation.

If you keep all of the actions just described in mind, you should start to see an improvement on your FICO score. You can also go to www.myfico.com to use a simulator that will show you how to improve your score in your particular situation.

KNOW WHAT YOU CAN AFFORD ON YOUR BIG PURCHASES

One of the main reasons that you want to have a good FICO score is to get the lowest interest rates possible when you need to finance large purchases such as a car and a house. But a good FICO score is not all it takes. You also need to know if you can afford the payments, month in and month out. Let's see if you can. You "played house" on pages 127–128 of Law 4. Now I want you to do the exercise below as well.

CALCULATING THE SIZE MORTGAGE
YOU CAN AFFORD

Your mortgage payment may be the highest known expense you will carry in a lifetime. You want to know that it is within your ability to pay it. In fact, ideally, you want to be able to pay it down faster than required. If you're buying a home (or even if you're simply curious about what size mortgage you could afford), you can turn the unknown into a known with relative ease. You only need to follow the steps below. But you should do this *before* you fall in love with a house that you just might not be able to afford, or before you talk yourself into buying something you may not be able comfortably to pay for. Remember, the laws of money rest on honesty and self-awareness. You can create what you want and keep what you have, as long as you base your actions on knowledge of what you can really afford instead of simply on what you want to have.

FIND YOUR MAXIMUM MONTHLY
MORTGAGE PAYMENT

1. Calculate your current net monthly income after taxes, Social Security contributions, retirement contributions, and all other automatic withdrawals from your paycheck. Write that figure here:

Figure 1 _____

2. Total the monthly payments on all your debts—include car payments, credit card payments, personal loans, and student loans. (Don't include mortgage payments or rent.) Be honest! Write the total here:

Figure 2 _____

If figure 2 equals more than 30 percent of figure 1, stop right here. (Multiply figure 1 by 0.3 to get 30 percent.) You are not currently in a financial position to own a home comfortably. You must first reduce your debt.

3. Find the sum that represents your monthly living expenses on page 256. Include food, transportation, gasoline, haircuts, dental, education, utilities, insurance—in other words, any regular bills that you pay, *excluding* the amount of your current rent or mortgage payments but *including* your debt payments (figure 2). Write that figure here:

Figure 3 _____

4. Subtract figure 3 from figure 1. Write the result here:

Figure 4 _____

Figure 4 is the maximum monthly amount you currently can afford to spend on a mortgage payment plus property taxes, homeowner's insurance, maintenance, possible PMI costs, and the other hidden costs of home ownership.

Keep in mind that this formula does not account for the tax savings that owning a home will confer. You will want to figure those savings into your monthly calculations before you shop for a home. Since you will likely save on both your federal and state taxes, be sure to consult a tax advisor.

5. Subtract 25 to 35 percent from figure 4 (multiply figure 4 by 0.35). Write the result here:

Figure 5 _____

Figure 5 is the highest comfortable monthly amount you can currently afford for a mortgage payment alone. The rest of the money needs to go toward the home-owning costs listed above.

FIND YOUR MAXIMUM MORTGAGE

If you want to figure out the size of the mortgage you can afford based on your maximum monthly payment, keep in mind that the size of this mortgage will also depend on available interest rates at the time you apply. That said, there are two easy ways to get the information you need:

1. Consult one of the many online calculators that compute your maximum mortgage amount when you enter the variables requested. For a list of my favorites, go to my website, suzeorman.com.
2. Use the table below, which can give you a general idea. I have used a 30-year mortgage table for purposes of illustration. To find the current interest rates for 30-year fixed mortgages, look at the financial pages of a newspaper. Then in the first column find the rate closest to the current one. Using that rate, choose the dollar figure along the row closest to the amount you can afford to spend each month (figure 5 from the preceding exercise). Once you find it, look up at the number at the top of the column. This is the approximate amount of the mortgage that you can afford.

	$100,000	$150,000	$200,000	$250,000	$300,000	$350,000	$400,000
6 %	600	899	1,199	1,499	1,799	2,098	2,398
6.5%	632	948	1,264	1,580	1,896	2,212	2,528
7 %	665	998	1,331	1,663	1,996	2,329	2,661
7.5%	699	1,049	1,398	1,748	2,098	2,447	2,797
8 %	734	1,101	1,468	1,834	2,201	2,568	2,935
8.5%	769	1,153	1,538	1,922	2,307	2,691	3,076
9 %	805	1,207	1,609	2,012	2,414	2,816	3,218

KNOW IF YOU CAN AFFORD TO RETIRE

Buying a home is not the only big event in your life for which you need to know what you can afford. You also need to know if you can afford to retire. In the worksheets on pages 251–258 of the guidebook, you figured out how much money you currently need each month to live, and how much money you have coming in to pay for those needs. When you retire (or want to retire), however, your income and expenses will change. It's important for you to figure out how much you expect to have when that happens.

When the time comes for you to think about retirement, fill out the next worksheet. You need to know what you can expect financially, and this exercise will help you do that. Use the figures from pages 251–258 to help you with the numbers below. Some categories will decrease on retirement; others, such as vacations, may increase.

MY EXPECTED RETIREMENT EXPENSES

	MONTHLY AVERAGE
Mortgage/rent	
Property taxes	
Home maintenance, association or condo fees	
Utilities (gas, electric, oil, water)	
Telephone, cellular phone, cable	
Home systems (alarm, pool, spa, cleaning service)	
Garden, firewood, lawn care	
Food, alcohol, restaurants, home entertaining	
Medical, dental, optometry	
Veterinarian	
Insurance (life, health, auto)	
Auto	
Transportation, parking, tolls	
Clothes, shoes, jewelry	
Dry cleaning/laundry service	
Hair, manicure, facial	
Alimony, child support	
Children's education	

	MONTHLY AVERAGE
Job training, education	
Income taxes on interest and dividends	
Professional fees (legal, accounting, counseling)	
Safe deposit box	
Technology (computer, printer, DSL)	
Credit card payments, loans (other than mortgage)	
Bank/credit union fees	
Postage, shipping	
Entertainment (video rentals, movie tickets, etc.)	
Recreation (sporting events, vacations, hobbies, clubs)	
Donations	
Gifts	
Lottery	
Cigarettes	
ATM cash withdrawals	
Seasonal expenses: firewood, furnace cleaning, summer camp	
Weekly expenses: lessons, cleaning help, babysitter	
Miscellaneous	
Total expected average monthly expenses	$

KNOW YOUR INCOME

In the next worksheet, record every source of income and the projected amount you expect when, in fact, you retire. You may want to follow the instructions on page 257.

MY EXPECTED YEARLY RETIREMENT INCOME

Pension checks after taxes and deductions	
Predictable bonuses off of past work income	
Social Security income	
Disability income	
Alimony and child support	
Bond income (outside of retirement accounts)	
Interest income (outside of retirement accounts)	
Dividend income (outside of retirement accounts)	
Rental income (that is expected to continue throughout retirement)	
Yearly gifts from any source	
Loan repayments	
All income from retirement accounts (assume that you have invested all your retirement account moneys at the going five-year CD rate)	
Miscellaneous	
Total Yearly Income	$
Monthly Income (Yearly divided by 12)	$

KNOW WHERE YOU STAND AT RETIREMENT

Let's see what the information you've just gathered means. In the worksheet below, write your Expected Monthly Retirement Income in the first row. Write the Expected Monthly Retirement Expenses figure (page 276) in the second row. Subtract the expenses from the income. Write the resulting figure in the "Difference" row. This figure is the amount of your monthly deficit or excess.

Expected monthly retirement income	$
Expected monthly retirement expenses	$
Difference (monthly expected deficit or excess)	$

Expected Deficit

Let's say that your expected retirement expenses are $3,000 a month and that your expected income is only $2,300 a month. This leaves you $700 a month short to meet your expenses. At this point you may decide that you cannot currently afford to retire. At least you now know, but to take action, look again at your expenses. Start saving at the rate you need to.

SAFEGUARD WHAT YOU NEED

If you are a few years away from retirement and the exercise above showed that you have just enough to be able to retire, I want you to do something. If you based your expected income numbers on money that is currently invested in the stock market and you are planning to put that money into bonds when you retire, you need to do so now. For instance, suppose you now know that the money in your retirement account is going to generate $700 a month in income. If you know that you will *need at least* that $700 a month (or whatever your figure is) for you to make it, you need to switch the funds from the unknowns of the stock market to the known of bonds.

In the example above, you need $8,400 ($700 × 12) a year income to make it. To ensure that you have that money secured, multiply the yearly amount you need from your account by 20 ($8,400 × 20 = $168,000) and transfer that amount into a safe investment right now. You need to put that money in a place where absolutely nothing could happen to it. That way, you would always have that money to generate the income you know you will need.

If you want it to be extra safe and sound, can you put more than that amount in very safe investments? Of course you can. But you have to have at least that much tucked away.

WHAT TO DO IF YOU HAVE MORE THAN YOU NEED

Let's imagine that when you moved $168,000 into bonds to ensure a safe, steady retirement income stream, you still had $132,000 in other liquid assets, for a total of $300,000. Your individual retirement asset allocation mix would now be 56 percent in safe bonds and 44 percent in whatever else you wanted. That "whatever else" can include stocks and mutual funds that will let your money grow, as long as you feel powerful about these decisions and they make sense financially.

This leads me to a crucial point: It is not your age that determines your personal retirement asset allocation mix when you have five or fewer years until retirement. Rather, it is how much you need to live on and how much money you currently have. As you can see, no one model works for everyone; but the principle of generating enough income so that you can cover your expenses does.

KNOW WHAT TO DO WITH YOUR "SAFE" MONEY

In this particular economic environment, you might want to consider investing any money you need to keep safe and sound in reliable vehicles. Please do not consider investing in bond funds, in most cases, and please don't invest in individual corporate bonds or preferred stock unless you are a very sophisticated investor.

Here are a few of the options you have for safe money:
* Treasury notes and bonds
* Ginnie Maes
* CDs
* Single-premium deferred annuities that guarantee an interest rate for the entire time the surrender charge is in force
* Insured municipal bonds (outside of a retirement account only).

PRIORITY CHECKLIST

I hope you've done a lot of the valuable work included in this section and in the Law 4 text of this book. To help get yourself on track and keep yourself there, use this checklist to log your progress. There's not an item on the list that you can afford to neglect, so don't stop until you can say yes and check off "Action taken" to every one.

HAVE YOU . . .	YES/NO	IF NOT, ACTION TO BE TAKEN	DATE BY WHICH I COMMIT TO ACTION	ACTION TAKEN ✓
Figured out how much money on average goes out every month?				
Figured out how much money on average comes in every month?				
Figured out how much debt you are carrying?				
Found out what your FICO score is and sought to improve it?				
Found the best interest rate for your credit debt?				
Begun paying down your credit card debts?				

HAVE YOU . . .	YES/NO	IF NOT, ACTION TO BE TAKEN	DATE BY WHICH I COMMIT TO ACTION	ACTION TAKEN ✓
Set up an emergency fund for at least eight months of income and begun to fill it?				
Established a line of credit sufficient for an emergency fund while you fill your own emergency fund?				
Made sure you have adequate health insurance?				
Begun paying an extra month's payment per year on your mortgage? *Or* Figured out how large a mortgage you could afford?				

HAVE YOU . . .	YES/NO	IF NOT, ACTION TO BE TAKEN	DATE BY WHICH I COMMIT TO ACTION	ACTION TAKEN ✓
Figured out where you stand and where you want to stand in regard to stock market investments?				
Found out exactly what your retirement benefits are and how they will work?				

You now know the actions that you have to take to have the power over the knowns in your financial life and the unknowns. As you take responsibility for knowing what you have and providing for what you don't know, you are changing your future and your loved ones' futures for the better. This is hard, nuts-and-bolts work of the laws of money. But there's another side to the story—one that has more to do with your mental attitude than action—and that's what you'll put to use in the final section of this guidebook, Law 5: "Money Has No Power of Its Own."

GUIDE TO LIVING LAW 5:

MONEY HAS NO POWER
OF ITS OWN

This is the final law of money. Even if you have not been able to complete all the exercises in this guidebook, I think that you will find that the laws themselves are already at work in your life. Just by bringing the truth of these laws into your awareness, your life and your perspective on money begin to change. You start to create harmony between yourself and your money, as well as a sense of equanimity that can eventually permeate your entire life.

Law 5 asks you to think about what is true for you, what is true for your money, and what is power *really*? In particular it asks you to consider power in relation to your money. As I said in the text, Law 5 is different from all the others. It has to do with your attitude rather than your actions. But please understand this: your actions—all of them—come from your mental attitudes about who you are and what you have. The way you think about yourself, your life, and your money determines which actions you take with your money; your actions in turn will determine your financial destiny. You are the source of your money's power, you define your money; it does not define you. Remember the story of my penny pit. Money is just money. It is a tool—inert until you bring your power, attention, and intention to it.

No matter how much or how little money you have, and no matter how much debt you are carrying right now, you still have the final say on how much you need and how you handle what you have. You can't drive your financial life to where you want it to go if you take your hands off the steering wheel and your foot off the accelerator. It really is that simple.

YOUR RELATIONSHIPS AND MONEY

In the text of Law 5, we explored the relationship that you have to your own power as well as how you apply that power to your own money. But you do not live in this world as an isolated human being. You live in this world every day surrounded by many people who also deal with money. Over your lifetime, you will form vital relationships with some of these people—your parents, spouse or life partner, kids, siblings, friends, employer, and employees.

Even though you are the power behind your money, if the people in your life are breaking the laws of money, you will become a victim of their behavior. Please pay attention to what I say here: If you link yourself to people who are breaking the laws of money, *you* will eventually pay a price. This section of the guidebook is designed to help you understand your own power and especially how it operates in relationships. I want you to protect your power and your money against potential losses from relationships with financial lawbreakers.

WHAT IS A POWERFUL RELATIONSHIP?

Think back to the story of Lee and Walter. Lee came to understand that she is as strong and accomplished with Walter as she is without him. Her ability to exercise her power to build a stronger financial future did not depend on what Walter had or what he wanted. She learned who she is—with or without money.

Walter, on the other hand, seems to have allowed his money to define him. He may believe that his personal power stems entirely from his money, and not the other way around.

How much of what is going on with Walter and Lee's power struggle is happening in your relationships as well?

YOUR EXERCISE

Ask yourself these questions. Be completely honest with yourself as you consider whether to circle yes or no.

1. If you had more money than you do right now, would you actually have more personal power in your relationship than you currently do? Yes / No
2. If you had less money than you do right now, would that make you less personally powerful in your relationship than you currently are? Yes / No
3. Do you think that, because your spouse or life partner makes more money than you, he or she has more power in your relationship? Yes / No

How did you answer the questions? I believe that the only right answer to any of these questions is no. But I also know that the whole world today is set up to lead you to think that the amount of money you have is the most important thing about you and that the money you make determines who is powerful in a relationship. Don't judge yourself harshly for needing to learn that this simply is not true.

However, if you still do feel that it is true, you may want to reread the text of Law 5. Please also practice the exercises in this fifth portion of the guidebook until the truth of the law—that money has no power of its own—becomes your own truth. You want this knowledge to become part of your attitude toward yourself, your money, and your relationships.

THE POWER STRUGGLE

Do you view the person with whom you are in a relationship as more like Lee or Walter?

Most relationships, regardless of the amount of money they actually involve, have some sort of power struggle or ongoing negotiation about money. More often than not we translate our feelings about money—and about ourselves and our loved ones—into some sort of monetary reward or punishment. We tend to use money to exert control. If you link yourself with someone who makes a substantially different level of money than you or who has a different sense of self from you, you may eventually have a conflict, especially if the other person doesn't understand that money has no power of its own.

I know that this can be a thorny problem. Because of your own understanding of money and your view of your own personal power, you may have to rethink long-term close relationships and relate to people in new ways. But unless you take responsibility for your associations and how they can affect your financial life—unless you pay close attention to this fifth law—you may find yourself in financial trouble. This law will be at work in your life even when you are not conscious of it. That's why you have to review and reflect on your relationships in the exercise that follows.

EASY TO SAY, NOT SO EASY TO DO

I can tell you how to deal constructively with any financial law-breakers in your life, but it won't be easy for you to take action. One of the hardest things to do is to tell someone you love that he has hurt or disappointed you, that she was not there when you needed her, or that his actions have had a direct effect on how you feel about him. After you reveal this to someone, you have to be ready to deal with a flood of emotions and work to set things right.

YOUR EXERCISE

Ask yourself: "Who in my life is breaking the laws of money? Could this person's actions affect who I am, what I have, and what I want?"

Could this person be your child? Your spouse or life partner? A good friend? Your parent? Your business partner or someone with whom you work closely? Be warned: When those to whom you are close are not telling the truth or living truthfully, they usually do not do what is right for themselves or their money—which means they cannot do what is right for you either.

Think this through carefully. Then list in the space provided the most significant people in your life—all of them—to whom this applies. If you are still breaking any of the five laws of money, you might also include your own name here—focusing on your problems in this context may help you weed out those last behaviors that keep you from living strictly by these laws. You need to be specific. Name names and state each person's relationship to you.

1. _____

2. _____

DON'T BALK THE TALK

One of the most important parts of any relationship is communication. The best, and often only, action you can take with a financial lawbreaker is to talk. And the best place to start what can be a difficult conversation is with your own experience, your own emotions, and your own attitudes. You may not be able to tell someone what he can or can't think, or what she should or shouldn't do, but you can certainly tell him or her how you feel. Here are some ways to do that:

> "When you don't let me move the furniture around in our apartment, it makes me feel as if I'm less important to you than these things."

> "When you don't tell me the truth about your debt and you spend money on nice gifts for me or luxury items for our family, I get very scared about our ability to work together as a couple and save for our goals and our retirement."

> "When you want me to quit my job and stay home, I feel like you don't value what I do or value who I am."

> "When you don't tell me about your financial trouble, I feel as if you don't trust me. Then I feel guilty—as if I've

done something to make you distrust me. I'd like to talk with you to try to figure out how you can trust me more."

As you can see, these are opening lines for a deeper discussion of the financial issues that concern you.

LET'S PLAY "HONEST FINANCIAL RELATIONSHIP"

In Law 4, you learned how to play house. You can use that same exercise to look at your relationships. In playing "honest financial relationship," you get in touch with how you feel and what you can and cannot afford to do *before* you venture into a difficult financial situation. The aim is that this play will turn a law-breaking association into a law-abiding, productive one.

In this exercise, I want you to plan just such a conversation that you need to have with a person whose name you have written down on page 288. Choose the one person from the list who has the greatest role in your life or effect on your life. This is the person who could cause the most damage emotionally and financially. Answer the questions below, immediately, truthfully, and without editing your thoughts:

Who is the person? _____

What is that person's relationship to you? _____

In your opinion, what laws of money is this person breaking? In what way is this happening? (You will notice that, when someone breaks one law, he or she usually breaks at least one other as well. That's why I have asked you to answer what laws this person is breaking.)

In my opinion, the laws of money that *[person's name]* is breaking are:

_____

_____

_____

_____

And this is how he or she is breaking them:

_____

_____

_____

_____

What effect is this person's lawbreaking having on your feelings and your financial situation?

_____

_____

_____

_____

In the space below, pretend you are initiating a conversation with this person and that you are telling him or her everything you have ever wanted to say about how he or she is breaking the laws. But please, before you say anything—or even write anything—you must *pass all your words and thoughts* through the three gatekeepers (see page 221): Is it kind? Is it necessary? Is it true? Okay, now with those gatekeepers in your head and your heart, please write below everything you want to say to that person.

_____

_____

_____

_____

Look at what you just wrote. Please reevaluate every word you wrote with the three gatekeepers *one more time*. Also look at what you wrote and see if you can find within the passage your own individual power words, which you created in the introduction to this guidebook. Try to remember those words and the questions you created around them and please write them in the spaces below.

_____

_____

_____

_____

_____

_____

Just to serve as a reminder here are the questions that I created in the introduction:

What is the **truth**?

What do I **have**?

What is **right** for me?

What is **known**?

What is **power**?

Again, before you proceed to take any action with the person to whom you want to talk, you need to make sure that you yourself are not about to break any of the laws. Make sure that what you have written is true. Go through the passage and answer all of your personal power questions. If everything feels, sounds, and looks right, you can proceed; if anything isn't right, go back and rewrite what you would like to say until it is right. You might just need to get some extra paper to do so, because you may need to go through several drafts.

Once you are clear within your own self about what you want to say, you are ready to go on to the next step. As you do so and as you make your playing of "honest financial relationship" real, I want you always to keep your power words and questions in mind. They will keep *you* centered and focused on your real goal here, which is not anger or recrimination, but truth and personal power.

NO MORE PLAYING; NOW MAKE IT REAL

Make a specific plan for getting this conversation to happen. If you cannot do it face to face, and you do not want to do this over the phone, you may decide to write a letter. I would suggest that you actually write the letter with a pen and paper and not on email. This will no doubt be a difficult subject to discuss—which is why you have not done so—and you want to make sure that you choose your words carefully. Again, you want to make sure that you yourself are not breaking any of the laws by what you say and how you say it. Sometimes, in email, statements can be misinterpreted and, because it is such a quick medium, people write and send messages in the heat of the moment that they may later wish they had not sent. You may end up writing several drafts of your letter and I suggest that you allow twenty-four hours to pass before you review it, edit one last time, and ultimately send it. You want this necessary process to be slow, deliberate, true and kind.

If you live with or in proximity to the person with whom you need to have the conversation, I still suggest that you review carefully what you wrote and give yourself at least a day to insure that you have in mind exactly what you want to say and how you want to say it. Before you broach this conversation face-to-face, here are some questions to think about.

When can you broach the subject?

_____

(Pick a time when you know that you and the other person will not be limited in the time you have to talk. You don't want to start this conversation just before you have to leave for work in the morning, for instance.)

Where would it be best to meet and talk?

_____

(Choose a location at which you won't be overheard or interrupted, and where both of you can feel free to express yourselves honestly.)

What do you want to happen?

_____

_____

_____

_____

(Do you want to help this person understand and grow closer to you? Do you want to put a stop to your involvement in the person's lawbreaking? Do you want to distance yourself from this person or stop your association altogether?)

What will you do if this person cannot or will not listen to you? What would be right for you?

_____

_____

_____

_____

This last is the hardest question to answer honestly. Generally speaking, blood relatives are yours for life, but that doesn't mean you have to involve yourself financially or emotionally in their lawbreaking. But what will you do if your spouse or partner won't listen to you? If it's a lifelong friend or a close neighbor?

You may have to give the person a little time for the truth of what you're saying to sink in. You may have to seek professional help to sort out your own liability. You may have to limit your contact with the person. Or you may have to consider severing the connection in some personal or legal way. Once again, you need to remember that only you can do what is right for you.

You can repeat this process as often and with as many people as you need to in order to sort out your financial relationships and to reestablish your power over who you are and over your money. The most important thing is that you actively choose whom you let into your life and whom you keep out.

— —

THE DOS AND DON'TS OF BEING A FINANCIAL GROWN-UP

Before you complete this law, I want to assure you that all your efforts to change your financial life are having and will continue to have a good effect on your financial life. You may feel that it's a lot to take in. You may think that you still have a long way to go before you are living the laws daily. That's okay. Life is a process. The point is to make sure that we're making progress in the right direction. You want to be sure you're growing, not just going.

Consider this. Just as some people don't look their chronological age—they either look a lot younger or a lot older than they are—some people don't act their age when it comes to money. When you live the laws of money, you act like a financial grown-up, and that means you keep what you have and create what you deserve. Do you know your financial age? When it comes to investments, do you feel like a baby or do you get the information you need and make confident decisions? When you look into the future, do you panic or do you figure out what you need and start making provisions? Are you expecting someone to take care of you, or do you knowingly think and act on your own behalf?

If you're in doubt about your financial age, read through the Dos and Don'ts that follow here. The more your financial actions line up with the Dos and steer clear of the Don'ts, the more growing up you've done in regard to your financial life.

DO...	DON'T...
1. Tell the truth about your money.	1. Let money become your badge of success.
2. Know what you have now.	2. Live in the past.
3. Know and accept who you are.	3. Compare yourself to others.
4. Invest mainly in the knowns first.	4. Act out of fear or hope.
5. Plan for the unforeseen.	5. Do something you don't like or understand with your money.
6. Get out of debt.	6. Be an all-or-nothing investor.
7. Make your financial decisions in tune with your time of life.	7. Trust others more than you trust yourself.
8. Keep good financial company.	8. Be an accomplice to financial lawbreakers.
9. Stay in touch with your current financial reality.	9. Ride on past financial decisions.
10. Respect your priorities.	10. Betray your own values.

The Bottom Line

We've almost come to the end of the guidebook of *The Laws of Money*. I hope this section has helped you see both how personal and how universal these laws and their applications are. I also hope that you have learned many new ways to manage your own power over your money and your life.

None of the laws of money stands alone. Each one builds on and grows from the others. You need to put *all* five laws into action to make your financial footing strong.

As a way of reinforcing the laws in your thinking and actions, I want you to make sure you've completed all the exercises in this guidebook. If you find you haven't, please make an appointment with yourself on your calendar to finish them. Give yourself a deadline for doing each one. Besides writing this in your calendar, I also want you to write your deadline date in the outer margin of the page alongside the unfinished exercise and initial it. Mark each unfinished exercise with a colored stick-on flag, so that you can see the work you need to do even when your book is closed. Keep working on your exercises and deadlines until you've completed the work and can honestly remove every one of the flags.

Finally, there is a recap of the five laws. After you have looked back over the work you've done in this guidebook and have read the recaps, please take the time to write a paragraph on what you have learned about each so far. Then write another paragraph about what actions each law calls for in your life right now. Even though you will eventually complete all the exercises in the guidebook, you will always want to keep the laws of money in mind as you re-create yourself and your financial life in the days, months, and years to come. The more you think about the laws and write down how you see them applying to your life, the more they will become a natural part of your thoughts and actions.

LAW 1: TRUTH CREATES MONEY, LIES DESTROY IT

Only you can decide to stop lying about your money—by spending more than you earn, or by pretending to others that you have more than you do—and only you can start telling nothing but the truth.

This is what this law has taught me:

_____

_____

_____

_____

_____

And this is how I will put those teachings into action:

_____

_____

_____

_____

_____

LAW 2: LOOK AT WHAT YOU HAVE,
NOT AT WHAT YOU HAD

Only you can decide to let go of your financial past, look at what you have today, and take action.

This is what this law has taught me:

_____

_____

_____

_____

_____

And this is how I will put those teachings into action:

_____

_____

_____

_____

_____

_____

LAW 3: DO WHAT IS RIGHT FOR YOU *BEFORE* YOU DO WHAT IS RIGHT FOR YOUR MONEY

Only you have what it takes to become honest and secure with who you are. Once you are honest and secure with yourself, only you can always do what is right for you *before* you do what is right for your money.

This is what this law has taught me:

_____

_____

_____

_____

_____

_____

And this is how I will put those teachings into action:

_____

_____

_____

_____

_____

_____

LAW 4: INVEST IN THE KNOWN
BEFORE THE UNKNOWN

Only you can decide how to invest your money and take action to protect your life and your money. Only you can make sure that you've done all that you can with your money to protect it, you, and your loved ones against unforeseen, unknown events. You do this by investing first in the knowns of your life.

This is what this law has taught me:

_____

_____

_____

_____

And this is how I will put those teachings into action:

_____

_____

_____

_____

_____

_____

LAW 5: MONEY HAS NO POWER OF ITS OWN

Only you have what it takes to make your life powerful, to make your money grow, to create what you deserve, and to keep what you have.

This is what this law has taught me:

_____

_____

_____

_____

_____

And this is how I will put those teachings into action:

_____

_____

_____

_____

_____

_____

_____

PUTTING ALL THE LAWS TO WORK FOR YOU

The main goal of the laws of money is to help you get out and stay out of financial trouble. But staying out of trouble is not enough; it is also essential that you use these laws to help build a life you deserve. Staying out of trouble is fairly easy, but realizing what it is that you believe you deserve and being able to create that can be harder.

So, I have another question for you:

WHAT DO YOU BELIEVE YOU DESERVE?

In the space below, please make a list of everything that you believe you deserve in your life:

_____

_____

_____

_____

_____

_____

Now, how do you make what you believe you deserve a reality? Please look at the following words:

Create what you deserve!

Study them for a second.

The two key words that I want you to note are "create" and "deserve." It is one thing to know what you deserve (which you have now indicated above). It is another to know what actions you must take so that you can bring what you believe you deserve into your life. Nothing in your life is going to come to you just because you feel you deserve it or because you feel you are owed it. Life is not that easy or that fair. You have to ask yourself what *you* owe your *life*, not what your life owes you.

What actions are you going to take to make sure that *you create* all that you believe you deserve?

Please copy the list of what you deserve into the next worksheet. In the second column, write all the actions that you have to take—and are going to take—so that you make that wish list a reality.

WHAT I BELIEVE I DESERVE	WHAT ACTION I HAVE TO TAKE TO CREATE THAT WHICH I DESERVE

Keep this list handy and check it every so often to see if you really are taking the actions that you need to. If you aren't—if you're delaying, or if you're telling yourself you no longer can get what you deserve—ask yourself why. What's holding you back? Go through the exercises in the guidebook again to see if you may need to take other actions to make the ones in this last worksheet effective.

THE LAWS AND THE WORLD

I love these laws of money and I believe from the deepest part of my soul that you can take them to heart as I have and live your life by them. I believe that they have helped me and that they can help you become a better person in all that we do—in our personal lives and in our financial lives. Through our actions and beliefs, we can make this world a better place. And isn't it true that our world needs our blessings, our particular greatness more than ever? Our role as beings on this planet is to keep our thoughts, actions, and energy grounded in truth. This is our role as financial beings, as well. As individuals and as a nation, we must learn to come from the place of truth, and to know that power is not created by anything but truth. In this way, we will create goodness, money, and authentic power. We will create what we all deserve.

IT IS ALL IN YOUR HANDS NOW

It is amazing to look back over your life and see how much you have changed both physically and financially, isn't it? Whenever I am around young kids, I like to get down on the ground with them, take one of their little hands in mine, and say to them, "Look at your hand. Look at your fingers." Then I put their little palm against mine, patty-cake style, and say, "My hand used to be as small as yours and now look at it." They usually stare while I continue: "The same thing will happen to you, as you get older. You will get bigger and everything about you will change. So you have to try to remember that even though your hand is so little right now, and sometimes it may be hard for you to grab and hold on to all that you want, as you get older your hand and your five fingers will get just as big as mine are today. And your hands are all that you will ever need to go out there and create everything you deserve." Of course, most of the kids gaze back at me with a blank stare or a puzzled look, as if they do not believe that they are really going to get older and as if they are wondering, Why is this woman telling me this?

But we all do get older, don't we? Even as an adult, before you got to know the five laws of money, you just might have been handling your financial life with hands that were the size of a five-year-old's. You might have been finding it hard to get and hold on to things you wanted. The bottom line is that these five laws, like your five fingers, can become a conscious part of you and help you in everything you do:

✦   Know that truth really is the only path that leads to wealth.

✦   Know and appreciate what you have.

✦   Know which actions are good for you.

✦   Know how to protect what you have and increase what you want.

✦   Know that you are more powerful than your money.

Is it that simple? You bet it is. Just as your fingerprints are unique to you, so are the life lessons that come to you every day through the decisions you make and live with your money. When you are guided by these five laws, you can make the right decisions and take the right actions for yourself and your money. And you will live the life you deserve.

Now you go out there and make it happen!

INDEX

family, communicating about
    money with, 27–29, 70
Fannie Mae, 126
fantasy, living in, 71–72
fear:
  absence of, 22
  exercise, 193–97
  of loss, 40–41
Fear Factor Scale, 74, 79–84, 240
Federal Reserve Board, 39
fed fund rate, 147–48
FICO score, 99–101, 129–30,
    266–70
financial advisor:
  communication with, 21
  roles of, 4–5
  and stock market, 18–19,
    139–40
financial age, 296–97
financial challenges, 8–9
financial fingerprints, unique,
    55–56
financial flight, 170
financial goals exercise, 183–84
financial grown-ups, 296–97
financial information, sources of,
    19
financial lawbreakers, 163–64,
    288–90
financial lifeboat, 185–86
financial situation:
  assigning blame for, 207
  challenges in, 8–9
  changing perspectives in, 48–49
  crossroads charts for, 198–207
  current, 44–45, 223–28
  denial of, 40
  fiscal cure for, 59–61

history of, 10–12, 16–17
ownership of, 73
past mistakes, 214–21
taking responsibility for, 21–22,
    207–8
warnings about, 67
what is right for you, 54–56
first financial impressions, 2–3, 8,
    22
first impressions, 1–3, 188–89
foreclosure, 107, 124
401(K) plans, 112–13, 149–50
Freddie Mac, 126
future, stealing from, 86–87

G

gap insurance, 117
gatekeepers, 221–23
getting what you deserve, 169–70,
    304–6
God permits U-turns, 20–21
grace, 169–70
grace period, 103
graven images, 47
Greenspan, Alan, 39
Guidebook, 177–308
  action plan, 247–48
  balance, 235–40
  bottom line, 298–306
  communication, 289–90,
    293–96
  create or increase your excess,
    259–61
  credit card debt, 262–65, 267
  crossroads charts, 198–207
  current assets and investments,
    240–42

ABOUT THE AUTHOR

———◆———

Suze Orman is the author of four consecutive *New York Times* bestsellers, *The Laws of Money, The Lessons of Life, The Road to Wealth, The Courage to Be Rich, The 9 Steps to Financial Freedom,* and the national bestsellers, *You've Earned It, Don't Lose It* and *Putting the 9 Steps to Work.* She is the personal finance editor on CNBC, the host of her own national CNBC-TV show that airs every weekend called *The Suze Orman Show.* Suze recently garnered an American Women in Radio and Television (AWRT) Gracie Allen Award for *The Suze Orman Show* in the National/ Network/ Syndication Talk Show category. The Gracies™ recognize the nation's best radio, television, and cable programming for women. Suze wrote, coproduced, and hosted four PBS pledge shows based on her best-selling books, which are among the most successful fund-raisers in the history of public television. In April 2004, PBS will start to air a special weekly edition of *The Suze Orman Show*. Suze is also a contributing editor to *O, The Oprah Magazine*.

Suze has been called a "force in the world of personal finance" and a "one-woman financial-advice powerhouse" by *USA Today*. Profiled in *Worth* magazine's hundredth issue (October 2001) as among those "who have revolutionized the way America thinks about money," Suze was also named in 1999 one of *Smart Money* magazine's top thirty power brokers, defined as those who have most influenced the mutual fund industry.

A 2003 inductee into the Books for a Better Life Award's Hall of Fame in recognition of her ongoing contributions to self-improvement, Suze had previously received the 1999 BBL Motivational Book Award for *The Courage to Be Rich*. In 2002, as a tribute to her ongoing involvement, the BBL organization established The Suze Orman First Book Category to honor a first-time author of a self-improvement book in any category. Also in 2002, Suze was selected as one of five distinguished recipients of the prestigious TJFR Group Business News Luminaries Award, which honors lifetime achievement in business journalism. In 2003, Suze received a Crossing Borders Award from the Feminist Press, which recognizes a distinguished group of women who not only have excelled in remarkable careers, but have also shown great courage, vision, and conviction by forging new places for women in their respective careers.

Suze directed the Suze Orman Financial Group from 1987 to 1997 and served as vice president–investments for Prudential Bache Securities from 1983 to 1987, where she became a CFP® professional. From 1980 to 1983, she was an account executive

at Merrill Lynch and from 1973 to 1980, a waitress at the Buttercup Bakery in Berkeley, California.

A sought-after speaker, Suze Orman has lectured widely
throughout the United States, Asia, and South Africa, helping
people change the way they think about money.

For more information about Suze, go to SuzeOrman.com.